Falling Pieces
of the
Broken
Sky

Falling Pieces of the Broken Sky

◆◆◆◆ JULIUS LESTER

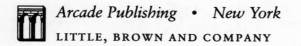
Arcade Publishing • *New York*
LITTLE, BROWN AND COMPANY

FIRST EDITION

Some of these essays, or portions of them, appeared in radically different form in the following publications: *Texas Observer, Amherst News, Parent's Choice, World Order, New York Times Book Review, New York Times* (op-ed page), *Horn Book, democracy, The New Republic, Boston Globe, Dissent, Mark Twain Journal, Salmagundi, Katallagete,* and *Tikkun.*

Copyright acknowledgments appear on page 278.

Library of Congress Cataloging-in-Publication Data
Lester, Julius.
    Falling pieces of the broken sky / Julius Lester. — 1st ed.
      p.   cm.
    ISBN 1-55970-059-9
    1. United States — Race relations. 2. Afro-Americans — Social conditions — 1975- 3. United States — Social conditions — 1945-
I. Title.
E185.615.L474 1990
305.8'00973 — dc20

                                           90-30427
                                              CIP

Published in the United States by Arcade Publishing, Inc., New York, a Little, Brown company.

10 9 8 7 6 5 4 3 2 1

BP

Published simultaneously in Canada
by Little, Brown & Company (Canada) Limited

Printed in the United States of America

The entire Universe will be broken into a thousand pieces in the general ruin, . . . chaos will return and will vanquish the gods and men, . . . the Earth and Sea will be engulfed by the Planets wandering in the Heavens. Of all the generations, it is we who have been designated to merit this fate, to be crushed by the falling pieces of the broken sky.

SENECA

CONTENTS

❖ ❖ ❖ *Falling Pieces of the Broken Sky*

Writers and
Writings

Henry Miller
(1891–1980)
✧✧✧

The passing of youth is marked by many events. For those of us who love literature, the deaths of literary mentors whose books gave us words by which to nurture ourselves during the dark nights of adolescence (and beyond) are losses whose sharpness is only a little less than the loss of a parent. Such a one was Henry Miller to me.

My adolescence coincided with the fifties. I was eleven when the decade began and turned twenty-one during the first month of the first year of the sixties. For those of us who slouched from adolescence to young adulthood in the fifties, it was, for the most part, a time when joy was tinged with nameless (and thereby all the more fearful) anxieties because of a man from Wisconsin named Joe McCarthy who saw Communists behind the elm trees on Main Street — and that was confirmed on "I Led Three Lives for the FBI," which we watched on newly acquired television sets. In school we were told that communism would bury us, and I wondered if Communists were morticians. Adolescence is a fearful enough time without the hysteria of national paranoia.

I entered college in the fall of 1956, and certainly by the beginning of my sophomore year I had read a reference to Henry Miller's *Tropic of Cancer,* the banned classic of pornography available only in Paris. I fantasized about going there and buying a copy of it (and that other banned classic, *Lady Chatterley's Lover*) and smuggling them past Customs wrapped in brown paper.

The very name, Henry Miller, was a rebuke to Senator McCarthy and J. Edgar Hoover, even if I had to settle for reading *Big Sur and the Oranges of Hieronymus Bosch* as my introduction to him. Reading anything by Henry Miller was to strike a blow for freedom. At least that's how it felt at age nineteen.

Miller did not disappoint, however. He wrote not of security but risk. He was scornful of conformity as a principle on which to base the good life. "One's destination is never a place but rather a new way of looking at things," he wrote in *Big Sur.*

It was that "new way of looking at things" I so desperately wanted, that I so desperately needed. If the fifties were a time when one kept careful vigil over his thoughts lest he speak and reveal himself to be un-American, how was I, a black adolescent, supposed to find coherence in a society that regarded me as more than an ape but less than a human being? And what was coherence when a black man could be lynched for a casual glance at a white woman? (That still happened during my adolescence in the South.)

"To detach yourself from your problems, that is the idea," Henry Miller wrote. "Why try to solve a problem? *Dissolve it!* Bathe it in a saline solution of neglect, contempt and indifference" (ibid.).

Through Henry Miller I learned that I did not have to allow myself to be defined by the sociopolitical reality. He glorified the physical — bones, flesh, blood, penis, feces, urine, toenails, body hair. Ideas had substance only when they were "wedded to action; if there is no sex, no vitality in them, there is no action. Ideas cannot exist alone in the vacuum of the mind. Ideas are related to living: liver ideas, kidney ideas, interstitial ideas, etc." (*Tropic of Cancer*).

Miller's words were like demons reaching out and grabbing my hand, pulling my hair, and biting me on the neck.

The earth is not an arid plateau of health and comfort, but a great sprawling female with velvet torso that swells and heaves with ocean billows; she squirms beneath a diadem of sweat and anguish. Naked and sexed she rolls among the clouds in the violet light of the stars. All of her, from her generous breasts to her gleaming thighs, blazes with furious ardor. She moves amongst the seasons and the years with a grand whoopla that seizes the torso with paroxysmal fury, that shakes the cobwebs out of the sky; she subsides on her pivotal orbits with volcanic tremors. She is like a doe at times, a doe that has fallen into a snare and lies waiting with beating heart for the cymbals to crash and the dogs to bark. Love and hate, despair, pity, rage, disgust — what are these amidst the fornications of the planets? (ibid.)

Miller wrote with the fury of Nature, and refused to be embarrassed by our clumsy and perishable physicality. Instead he exalted it into a psalm and I understood that if I equated whiteness with being human (and being black, I knew that was a failed equation), then my algebra would be flawed if, in a desperate attempt at salvation, I equated blackness with being human.

"When you're right with yourself it doesn't matter what flag is flying over your head or who owns what or whether you speak English or Monongahela" (*The Colossus of Maroussi*).

Or whether you are white or black.

Robert Hayden

(1913–1980)

✧✧✧

When I entered Fisk University in the fall of 1956, he had been there ten years already, an associate professor in the English department. That he was a poet was of no consequence to his colleagues or the administration. "They don't even know what a poet is," he would complain to me in later years.

Once, when a volume of his poems was published, the chairman of the English department, who was white, commented: "Your poems are too often about race. You should write on the more universal themes."

The first time I saw Robert Hayden, my overwhelming impression was of a great and weighted loneliness. He was walking alone in the dusk of an autumn evening past the grove of magnolia trees that stood then in front of Livingstone Hall, the freshman boys' dormitory. His head was bent to one side as if he were hanging from some invisible gallows. In his right arm, books were cradled against his chest. He walked rapidly, nervously, and though I had heard only his name from upperclassmen, I knew: "That's Mr. Hayden."

The loneliness I sensed about and in him was an intimation of the loneliness about which he would seek to educate me, for it was the particular loneliness of the black creative artist.

Anaïs Nin, in the fourth volume of her *Diaries,* quotes Richard Wright as telling her: "As a writer here I am strangled by petty humiliations, and daily insults. I am obsessed with only one theme. I need perspective. I need to get away from personal hurts, my personal irritations. I am so constantly disturbed I cannot even work. I need to live free if I am to expand as a writer."

Was that possible for a black writer, especially during Hayden's years at Fisk, in Nashville, Tennessee? The South was still segregated and to leave the campus and venture into town was to enter a surreal world in which your life was defined by signs designating the separate WHITE and COLORED sections on the bus, the separate water fountains in stores, the separate entrances at the railroad and bus stations, and the NO COLORED ALLOWED signs in the doors and windows of restaurants and coffee shops.

There was no confirmation of self as a black man by the wider society; there was no confirmation of self as a poet by the university. Somehow, Hayden maintained faith in his soul and his gift even while teaching fifteen hours of classes a week each semester — two sections of freshman English, sophomore humanities, early-twentieth-century American literature, and Victorian lit. If he wanted to, he could also offer a seminar in creative writing. It was not surprising that his migraine headaches put him to bed for days at a time.

He became one of my mentors, midwifing the writer in me but teaching me almost nothing about the craft of writing. "A person is either a writer or he isn't. And the only way to develop as a writer is rewrite, rewrite, rewrite." He was fond of telling how Dylan Thomas rewrote one of his poems seventy-five times.

But being a writer was not only a matter of talent. Whether that talent developed would be a matter of character, and who knew that better than he? Would I believe that poetry mattered if I had to write it while teaching five courses a semester, write it when few read it? I did not know.

I did not learn much in his classes because he taught literature I did not like — Henry James, American realism, and Victorian essays and poetry. My attitude showed and he attached a note to a paper I'd written for the Victorian-literature course.

Julius

I am upset by this "performance," because you are obviously the ablest and most original thinker in this class, not excluding the poor old baffled broken-down instructor. Yet you seem to be throwing everything you have away — or at least not using all your resources. Even this paper has gleams and flashes of wit and insight which do not appear on anyone else's. If I thought that giving you a D would make you perk up, believe me I'd slap one on you. But I know it wouldn't accomplish anything for you in your present state of mind. Whatever you may think of Victorian lit. as such, you must *not* commit the unpardonable (to me) "sin" of not using all your really superb gifts at *all times*. What is not used atrophies, as you well know.

Besides all this, I need your support in this and the other classes you have with me. When *you* of all people don't do your work you add to my feelings of frustration. Can you understand what I mean by this?

I understood that he was not only mentor; he was a person who needed to be given to and he needed me to give. While I had never thought of myself as an able or original thinker, and certainly not his superior in that regard, I was ashamed that I had been so irresponsible as not to consider the effect my attitude in the class would have on him. My negative attitude toward Victorian literature did not change, but I ceased putting it on exhibit.

He gave to me in a different way at the end of that year. To graduate, I had to pass comprehensive exams in English literature and American literature. Mr. Hayden supervised the latter.

I sat in the exam room looking at the questions Mr. Hayden had just passed out. Not only did I not know the answers; there was not one question that I understood! I consulted briefly with myself, and however many of me were present agreed that there was only one thing to do: write my name neatly on the cover of the blue book, hand it to Mr. Hayden, who was sitting at the head of the long conference table, and go walk in the sun.

Later that day, I saw him walking across campus. "Well, young man. You really did it this time," he said, almost gaily.

What could I say?

"I gave you a C," he continued. "If I flunked you and made you stay another year, you'd flunk next year, wouldn't you?"

That was true. Thus I graduated, not because I had earned my degree but because Mr. Hayden thought I was more than the sum of my academic performance.

I spent the next year living at home in Nashville, my parents indulging my unemployment while I wrote. After some months of sending out manuscripts and having them return in what seemed like the next mail, I concluded that I was not a writer and told Mr. Hayden so.

"You will always have doubts," he said after a long silence. "Doubting that you are a writer is part of being a writer." Maybe it was then he told me his story about Oscar Wilde, who said: "At ten I sat down to write. At eleven I put in a comma. At twelve I took it out. At one I put it back in and went to lunch."

I moved to New York in the spring of 1961 and would see Mr. Hayden briefly whenever I returned to Nashville to visit my parents, but I no longer wanted him as mentor because I needed to find my way on my own, and in any event, he had found others to mentor.

In May 1966, I was in Nashville for the staff meeting of the Student Nonviolent Coordinating Committee (SNCC), for whom I was working as a photographer. We had just elected Stokely Carmichael as the new chairman. Even we did not know that within a few short weeks Stokely would convulse America and usher in a new era with the cry of "Black Power!"

Mr. Hayden had already felt the heat of its approaching flames. At a writers' conference at Fisk a few weeks before, he had been attacked as an Uncle Tom by students and by other black writers because he insisted that he was a poet, not a black poet.

He had also just been awarded the Grand Prize for Poetry at the first World Festival of Negro Arts at Dakar, Senegal. That honor was not enough to offset the rejection and attack made on him at the conference.

I was scarcely seated in his living room that May afternoon before he went into a tirade against black nationalists. I listened again to words I had heard almost ten years before when I had sat in that living room as his student: "There's no such thing as Negro literature, or *black* literature." His voice was poisonous with scorn. "There's good literature and there's bad literature, and that's all!"

I couldn't understand why he was so vociferous in denying that he was a black poet. Wasn't he the man who had written "Middle Passage," "Frederick Douglass," "Homage to the Empress of the Blues," and "Runagate, Runagate," four of the finest poems in the English language about the black experience? Why didn't he want to admit that he was a black poet, just as his beloved Matthew Arnold was an English poet?

To be black and be a writer has always meant being associated with the "cause" of civil rights, however. It is your birthright, whether you want it or not. It has been the black writer's sentence to have his or her work judged more on the basis of racial content than artistic merit. This is because whites grant individuality only to whites. A black writer is a priest, offering absolution to whites or leading blacks to the holy wars.

The prevailing black aesthetic of the late sixties was summarized succinctly by West Coast black activist and political theoretician Ron Karenga, who wrote: "All art must reflect and support the Black Revolution and any art that does not discuss and contribute to the revolution is invalid. Black art must expose the enemy, praise the people and support the revolution." In other words, art should be the voice of political ideology, and the black artist must comply or find him- or herself with an indifferent white audience and no black one.

Hayden was not conceived or reborn in the womb of black power. Such thinking was not only repugnant to him; it was a direct assault on the human spirit and art.

By its very nature, art was revolutionary, he had taught me, because art sought to change the consciousness, perceptions, and very beings of those who opened themselves to it. The revolutionary nature of art was mortally wounded when it was twisted to conform to political prescriptions.

I found myself caught between what he had taught me and the new ethos. But on that May afternoon, I felt great pain for him because, of all people, he did not deserve public humiliation at the hands of blacks angered because he refused to lead them to the holy wars. The humiliation was compounded when Fisk University hired a black writer with the "proper" credentials as writer-in-residence. He did much to make Mr. Hayden's humiliation continual by discouraging students from studying with him. Thankfully, Mr. Hayden was invited to teach at his alma mater, the University of Michigan, which he did.

Robert Hayden refused to be defined by anything other than the demands of his craft. He was a man who honored language and submitted himself to its requirements, not those of any ideology. I remember him telling me that writing consisted of words: "That may seem obvious, but it isn't. You see, I assume that you have something to say. Writing is caring enough to say it as well as the talent God gave you will allow."

Because he loved language, each word in his poems is precise, so that the lines are so tightly compressed as to be unbearable.

> In sun-whetted
>   morning,
> the dropped gull
>   splayed
> on sand,

> wind
> picking at
>   its feathers.
>
> Over the headlong
>   toppling
> rush and leashed-back
>   mica'd
> fall of the sea,
>   gulls
> scouting and
>   crying.

He did not use language to indulge himself in "expressing his emotions" (something for which he scorned me if I came remotely close to such narcissism). He used language to create worlds and make us see, because the work of a poet should make us recognize that we gaze on the world with blind eyes and call what we see real.

He chose words with the care of a sculptor chipping into marble. In his poem "El-Hajj Malik El-Shabazz," he gave the most vivid historical portrait of Malcolm X in six brief lines:

> He X'd his name, became his people's anger,
> exhorted them to vengeance for their past;
> rebuked, admonished them,
>
> their scourger who
> would shame them, drive them from
> the lush ice garden of their servitude.

How long did it take him to find that line, "He X'd his name"? Such a simple, direct line, but it sets up reverberations that extend back to August 1619. The last stanza of the poem could serve as Malcolm's epitaph:

He fell upon his face before
Allah the raceless in whose blazing Oneness all
were one. He rose renewed renamed, became
much more than there was time for him to be.

I saw Hayden last in the midseventies. He called me one
Sunday afternoon and I went down to his room at the
Fifth Avenue Hotel. He and his wife, Erma, looked like a
young couple on their honeymoon. The recognition due
him had come with his election to the Academy of American Poets, and his appointment as Consultant for Poetry
to the Library of Congress, a position equivalent at the
time to poet laureate of America. And he and I took special delight in the fact that we each had had books nomi-
nated for the National Book Award in the same year.

Few contemporary poets knew the craft of poetry as
well as Hayden. He loved meter and could write in many.
He was always learning his craft, seeking ways to find that
elusive point where sound, rhythm, and sense converged
in the one right word in the right place in a line of poetry.

He was always open to the new. In 1958 I "discovered"
haiku and began studying and writing them. I showed
them to Mr. Hayden, and we talked about the form, which
I knew more about than he. A few months later, he handed
me some sheets of paper. On them were haiku he'd written. I read them and was disappointed. Their form was
haiku; the spirit was not. Mentor or not, poetry is poetry,
and I told him.

He was miffed, but he managed a dry laugh and said,
"Well, that's the last time I'll show you my poems."

It wasn't, but when his *Selected Poems* appeared, the four
haiku were included under the title "Approximations."

Hayden respected the demands of his craft. In so doing,
he could not be restricted to the black experience or per-

mit himself to be used as a pawn in some neo-medieval morality play. His insistence that he was not a black poet was not a denial of race. His poetry is proof that he never denied that. But he did not make the mistake of believing that the totality of his humanity could or should be expressed through something called blackness.

He knew that to insist upon a separate identity as a black writer would be to place himself in a literary ghetto where he would be considered good enough to be compared only to other black writers. But he was an American poet writing out of the totality of his life's experience, part of which was racial, just as Robert Lowell was an American poet writing out of his experience, part of which was as a Roman Catholic.

Hayden's religious faith as a Baha'i sustained and nurtured him through the long years of isolation, through the times of asserting his humanity in the face of whites and blacks who wanted to deny that to him. Being a Baha'i helped him maintain his center when men of lesser faith would have succumbed to bitterness and self-pity. It gave him the courage to withstand the migraines as well as the lesions inflicted on his soul; and it gave him the courage to be whom God intended him to be.

In the ninth part of the poem "Words in the Mourning Time," he wrote:

> We must not be frightened nor cajoled
> into accepting evil as deliverance from evil.
> We must go on struggling to be human,
> though monsters of abstraction
> police and threaten us.
>
> Reclaim now, now renew the vision of
> a human world where godliness
> is possible and man

is neither gook, nigger, honkey, wop, nor kike

but man

permitted to be man.

If we ever reach that time when man is permitted to be man, one of the reasons will be this man, Robert Hayden, who when pressed into terrifying corners of loneliness refused to capitulate to those who, in the screaming agony of their own pain and loneliness, could do nothing but return evil for evil.

Aldous Huxley
(1894–1963)

❖❖❖

*The Hindus reckon four ages — that of the
schoolboy; that of the married man living
in the world; that of that mature man who
withdraws into the forest and tries to
understand nature, things and his own
essence; that of the aged man who detaches
himself completely from desire and, though
living bodily, dwells in the eternity which
he perceives even in temporal things.*
LETTER FROM ALDOUS HUXLEY TO
PHILIPPE DUMAINE
April 23, 1945

It is the description of all our lives. We are given four
seasons, and the success or failure of our lives depends on
how well we live the demands of each season.

Aldous Huxley lived his four seasons with exceptional
grace. Known to the world as a writer, he is best remembered for his prophetic novel of 1932, *Brave New World*,
and *The Doors of Perception*, an account of his experi-
ments with hallucinogenics in the fifties. Huxley published
forty-seven books in his sixty-nine years, but none are adequate reflections of him, because he was more than the
sum of his words.

✧✧✧

One's ideal, I dare say, should be, not the
snail, but the slug — naked, not armoured.
Unless one is vulnerable, one probably
never learns to be strong.
TO MRS. FLORA STROUSSE
October 13, 1934

The task of the first half of life is to set up our tents in
the sandstorm. Our identity is established when we can
say, "I am a . . ." Teacher, bus driver, accountant is a way
of knowing ourselves before others. We must see ourselves
in clear relief, a part of the frieze of reality, but standing
out from it in strong, sculpted lines.

Huxley knew himself first as a writer and intellectual.
His fame began in the 1920s with his witty, cynical novels
about the postwar generation. *Crome Yellow, Antic Hay,*
Those Barren Leaves, and *Point Counter Point* were to
that generation what the songs of Bob Dylan were to the
sixties, reflections of "the life and opinions of an age
which has seen the violent disruption of almost all the
standards, conventions and values current in the previous
epoch" (letter to his father, November 26, 1923).

Yet, Huxley was dissatisfied with his novels. They were
novels of ideas in which the life of the mind was put forth
as the only one worth living. The heroes of Huxley's novels are half-human, intellects without emotions, able to
perceive the world but unable to experience it. He sensed
that this was only a part of the human reality.

The nonrational was absent from Huxley's novels, but
not from his life. As early as 1916, when he was twenty-
two, he wrote the following advice to his brother, Julian:
"The people that I propose you shall read are as follows:
Blake perpetually, with a foundation of Jacob Behman

[Jakob Böhme]; that will keep your religion all right, the importance of which I cannot overemphasize."

The journey toward wholeness involves ceasing to mistake fragments of ourselves for the whole, no longer exalting one aspect of our being above the others.

Huxley's emphasis on the mind was the proper task of the first season, and in 1919, in another letter to Julian, he wrote with the unself-conscious arrogance only allowed the young: "Great events are both terrifying and boring, terrifying because one may be killed and boring because they interfere with the free exercise of the mind — and after all, that freedom is the only thing in the world worth having."

Yet, the sense that he was defining only a corner of reality recurred five years later when he wrote his father: "A too early passion for reading detracts from the powers of observation and it is more important for the child to notice vividly what is going on outside him than to make him a precocious acquaintance with the inside of books." Only someone who knew little more than the "inside of books" would know this, and it indicated a growing tension in Huxley between his intellect and other ways of knowing, other realities.

A year later, in April 1925, came the first statement that the tension had been resolved — at least intellectually. In a letter to his close friend Robert Nichols, he wrote that

> the most vital problem is not the mental so much as the ethical and emotional. The fundamental problem is love and humility, which are the same thing. The enormous difficulty of love and humility — a difficulty greater now, I feel, than ever; because men are more solitary now than they were; all authority has gone; the tribe has disappeared and every at all con-

scious man stands alone, surrounded by other solitary individuals and fragments of the old tribe, for which he feels no respect. Obviously, the only thing to be done is to go right through with the process; to realize individuality to the full, the real individuality, Lao-Tz[u]'s individuality, the Yogis' individuality, and with it the oneness of everything. Obviously! But the difficulty is huge. And meanwhile the world is peopled with miserable beings who are neither one thing nor the other; who are solitary and yet not complete individuals; conscious only of the worst part of themselves . . . and devilishly proud of what they regard as their marvelous independence and their acuteness of spirit. For them love and humility are impossible. . . . What's to be done about it? That's the great question. Someday I may find some sort of an answer. And then I may write a good book, or at any rate a mature book, not a queer sophisticatedly jejune book . . . like all the blooming lot.

It was another ten years before Huxley began to say publicly what he wrote in this letter, and when he did, his contemporaries from the twenties could only wonder what had happened to the witty agnostic.

He had entered the second season.

✧✧✧

> *My besetting sin [is] the dread and*
> *avoidance of emotion, the escape from*
> *personal responsibility, the substitution of*
> *aesthetic and intellectual values for moral*
> *values — of art and thought for sanctity.*
> TO MRS. KETHVAN ROBERTS
> January 13, 1935

The seasons of our lives do not, like birthdays, come in neat succession. The human seasons overlap, and we glimpse the second and third while struggling to meet the demands of the first. Huxley's second season began in the midst of his first. It is generally that way with men because the second season is the one of marriage, of engaging the opposite.

In Huxley's essay on D. H. Lawrence, he quoted Lawrence on woman: "And God the Father, the Inscrutable, the Unknowable, we know in the flesh, in Woman. She is the door for our in-going and our out-coming. In her we go back to the Father; but like the witnesses of the transfiguration, blind and unconscious." These words describe the place Huxley's wife had in his life.

In 1919 he married Maria Nys, a young Belgian woman, who after thirty-two years of marriage wrote their son, Matthew, and wondered why Aldous had chosen her "out of the many prettier, wittier, richer, etc. young girls? Knowing all the time . . . that he could never teach me to write poetry or remember what I read in a book or spel [sic] or anything else he did set value on." But Aldous chose her precisely because she was his opposite — outgoing, at ease with people, intuitive, and spontaneous. Maria herself said that she was "his personal relationship interpreter," and Aldous called her his "dragoman," his guide.

Maria devoted herself wholly to Aldous and suffered for it. "I took over too much!" she wrote her daughter-in-law. Aldous's efforts to create relationships to the outside world ceased because Maria was there to do it for him; eventually, Aldous realized what had happened and began to make his own. By this time, however, Maria's sacrifice was almost total. While she was glad that Aldous "needs *no* interpreter ever now with human beings," she realized "it is a bit late for me to start training my mind in memorizing quotations which Aldous has at his fingertips." She admitted to her sister that she "suffered" because she hadn't developed her own abilities — or even lived her own life: "If I weren't married to Aldous, I would be a Catholic."

Her devotion to him did not stop, however. How could it? It was the only life she had known; and in 1954 when she learned she had terminal cancer, she refused to allow anyone to tell Aldous because, she explained, "My husband has a book to finish and must have peace of mind." During the months of her dying she worried that "it would be wrong for me to die before Aldous — I should have failed in my duty to him." And just as she had arranged Aldous's sexual liaisons throughout their marriage, in the face of death she found a woman she felt would be a good wife for him. Aldous married this woman, Laura Archera, a year after Maria died.

D. H. Lawrence was also indispensable to Huxley's journey toward wholeness. Huxley considered Lawrence "the most extraordinary and impressive human being I have ever known." Lawrence was Instinct as opposed to Huxley's Mind. Lawrence was violent in his opposition to the rational and scientific, preferring what he called "the dark loins of man." His influence on Huxley could be heard thirty-one years after his death and two years before Huxley's own in the London interview of 1961:

The blood and the flesh are there, and in certain respects they are wiser than the intellect. I mean if we interfere with the blood and the flesh with our conscious minds, we get psychosomatic trouble. But on the other hand, we have to do a lot of things with the conscious mind. I mean why *can't* we do *both* — we *have* to do both. This is the whole art of life: making the best of all the worlds.

What it means to make "the best of all the worlds" was expressed succinctly by Huxley in a letter to Julian in October 1946: "The unchanging essence of existence consists, in Vasily Rozanov's words, in 'picking one's nose and looking at the sunset.'"

Symbolic of Huxley's emergence from a wholly intellectual life was his love of warm climates. From 1923 until his death forty years later, he lived in southern Italy, southern France, and, from 1938, southern California. It was as if he had to be warm literally to become warm spiritually.

Another symbol of his learning to live anew was his learning to paint. Robert Nichols quoted him as saying:

It's so devilish exciting. And the discoveries one makes! Quite ordinary, of course — any painter who knows his job can put you up the wheeze. But the thing is to discover them for oneself. You can't imagine the lusciousness of putting on the paint. . . . Well, one day I discovered that if you waited till your paint was half-dry and then brushed it over — caressed it — with a dry brush, you got the most marvelous effects — a bloom! My dear Bob, I wouldn't have sold the excitement and the pleasure I had in making that discovery for a million pounds. Incredible!

He painted the physical world — trees, a seashell, a swing in a garden, as well as nudes and portraits. He was learning the physical world in its concreteness, as something alive in and of itself, and to use "the powers of observation" that had been neglected because of his own "too early passion for reading."

> *In spite of the appalling possibilities of unhappiness and the appalling frequency with which the possibilities are realized, I think on the whole it's most decidedly worthwhile — not for any good reason, of course; but for some mysterious good unreason.*
>
> TO MRS. FLORA STROUSSE
> January 28, 1930

It was not until December 1935 that Huxley's reading public became aware that the witty cynic had undergone a transformation.

On December 3, with war imminent in Europe, he made a public speech, something almost unprecedented for him at the time. In it he announced that he had become a pacifist.

> Our end is peace. How do we propose to realize this end? If we want to be treated with trust and affection by others we must ourselves treat those others with trust and affection. . . . We largely construct the ethical world in which we live. It is to a great extent a matter of choice whether we construct it as a world of fear and greed or as a world of trust and love. . . . there is nothing inherently absurd about the idea that the world which we have so largely constructed can also, if we so desire, be reconstructed on other and better lines.

. . . No end can be realized without appropriate
means. . . . No pacifist can permit himself to think in
abstractions. . . . war is a process of large-scale murder. . . . hostile nations consist of individual men and
women. . . .

There was nothing startling in these words. The shock
came when Huxley insisted that pacifism could not be
based on humanism

but in a spiritual reality, to which all men have access
and in which they are united. God . . . regarded, and
if possible experienced as a psychological fact, present at least potentially in every human being.
    If enough people address themselves to living up
to this belief, if enough people set out to experience
spiritual reality . . . then there will be peace; for
peace . . . is a by-product of a certain way of life.

This speech was a turning point in his life, and
Huxley ceased to be a clever writer and became a com-
passionate one.

Love, compassion and understanding or intelligence —
these are the primary values in the ethical system,
the virtues organically correlated with what may be
called the scientific-mystical conception of the world.
Ultimate reality is impersonal and non-ethical; but
if we would realize our true relations with ultimate
reality and our fellow beings, *we must practice
morality.*

The words are from *Ends and Means* (1937), and sur-
prisingly, this book had the same impact on that generation of students as his novels on the previous one.
    Huxley refused to align his pacifism with politics or

political action. In a letter to Kingsley Martin in 1938, he wrote:

> I become more and more firmly convinced that it is completely pointless to work in any field of politics . . . first, because one can't achieve anything unless one is in a key position, and second, because even if one were in a key position, all one could achieve would be, at the best, a deflection of evil into slightly different channels. . . .
>
> Religious people who think they can go into politics and transform the world always end up by going into politics and being transformed by the world. Religion can have no politics except the creation of small-scale societies of chosen individuals outside and on the margin of the essentially unviable large-scale societies.

When asked to sign a newspaper ad protesting the persecution of Jews in Germany, he refused, and in a letter to Jacob Zeitlin wrote:

> I don't see that any good would be done by my writing two or three thousand words on the subject. The persecution of the Jews in Germany is horrible in the extreme; but it is not by proclaiming the fact in a loud voice that this particular persecution will be stopped or that human beings will discontinue the habit of persecution, which is immensely old and which is bound up with habits of thought, feeling, action and belief, with traditional methods of social and economic organization such that, if the latter persist, the former must inevitably manifest itself. It is useless to treat small-pox by cutting out the individual pustules and stitching up the wounds.

In a letter to Julian in March 1941, he reduced his thinking to one sentence: "Saints would appear to be the only antidote to statesmen."

He had entered the third season, withdrawing "into the forest . . . to understand nature, things and his own essence." The third season brings wisdom, that ability to see into the heart of people and things without disillusionment about what is there. Wisdom is the smiling acceptance of what is, and Huxley had reached that place when, in 1941, he wrote: "We live under the illusion that all problems are at all times susceptible of a reasonably satisfactory solution. They are not."

Among the few who live the third season, there are two ways of doing it traditionally: the way of the sage and the way of the hero.

The sage is the one who, having penetrated to the heart of Being, remains there in silent communication with it. This is the way of the hermit and the monk. The hero goes to the heart of Reality but returns to the mundane world to offer what he knows to whomever will listen.

Huxley's way was the latter, and a prophetic note entered his writing. In 1946 he was predicting a world food shortage by the end of the century: "Power politics guarantees that the world shall *not* be fed properly." The same year, in a letter to Julian, he wrote that "oil will become a tool of international politics, as well as uranium if atomic energy is developed as a source of power."

In 1947 he wrote an essay, "The Double Crisis," that was one of the first on ecology.

Industrialism is the systematic exploitation of wasting assets. The thing we call progress is merely an acceleration in the rate of that exploitation. Such prosperity as we have known up to the present is the consequence of rapidly spending the planet's irreplaceable capital. . . .

Treat Nature aggressively, with greed and violence and incomprehension: wounded Nature will turn and destroy you. . . . if, presumptuously imagining that we can "conquer" Nature, we continue life on our planet like a swarm of destructive parasites — we condemn ourselves and our children to misery and deepening squalor and the despair that finds expression in the frenzies of collective violence.

While his vision penetrated into the future of the objective world, his hold on the inner one intensified and he did not despair at what he saw without.

My wife and I have just become grandparents. I wish the baby might have been born into a less dismal kind of a world; but perhaps it is no more dismal, after all, than it has always been. And in spite of all our efforts, we shall never succeed in making it undivine.

. . . we [can't] really be happy until we have nothing to rejoice at — nothing, that is to say, specifically *Ours*. Only then do we begin to have everything, impartially — the entire visible universe and the invisible too — being happy in all the countless reasons for happiness that exist in a world of infinite depth and beauty and significance, and not unhappy in our particular reasons for rejoicing, however compelling they may seem. But of course this is dreadfully easy to say, dreadfully hard to practise.

❖❖❖

> *God is even in one's own posterior when at*
> *last one has crawled full circle and seen it*
> *revealed in its full glory.*
> TO MRS. ELISE MURREL
> November 14, 1951

The fourth season of Huxley's life was marked by the
emergence of an ability to articulate the essence. It was
expression beyond the clever egocentricity of aphorism. It
was the kind of expression that comes when one is able to
gaze, unblinkingly, into the heart of darkness and the heart
of life.

On T. E. Lawrence: He is one of those great men for
whom one feels intensely sorry, because he was nothing but a great man.

On George Bernard Shaw: I have never found him
very interesting. Did he, after all, ever know anything about human beings?

On Timothy Leary: I spent an evening with him here
a few weeks ago [in 1962] — and he talked such
nonsense . . . that I became quite concerned. Not
about his sanity — because he is perfectly sane — but
about his prospects in the world; for this nonsense-
talking is just another device for annoying people in
authority, flouting convention, cocking snooks at the
academic world; it is the reaction of a mischievous
Irish boy to the headmaster of his school. One of
these days the headmaster will lose patience. . . . I
am very fond of Tim . . . but why, oh why, does he
have to be such an ass?

On Love [from a letter to his son on the dissolution
of the latter's marriage]: To become capable of

love — this is, of course, about two thirds of the battle; the other third is becoming capable of the intelligence that endows the love with effectiveness in an obscure and complicated and largely loveless world. It is not enough merely to know, and it is not enough merely to love; there must be knowledge-love and charity-understanding or prajna-karuna, in the language of Buddhism — wisdom-compassion. People have been saying this for the last several thousand years; but one has to make the discovery oneself, starting from scratch, and to find what old F. M. Alexander called "the means whereby," without which good intentions merely pave hell and the idealist remains . . . ineffectual, self-destructive and other-destructive. . . . It has taken me the greater part of a lifetime to begin to discover the immemorially obvious and to try, at least, to act upon the discovery. I hope it will take you only half a lifetime and that you will emerge from this excruciatingly educative ordeal with enough love and understanding to transfigure the second half.

On Reality: I hope and think that by awareness of what one is doing from moment to moment, one may be able to remain out of one's own light.

In February 1955, Maria died. As she lay on the threshold of eternity, Huxley showed that he dwelled "in the eternity" that can be perceived "even in temporal things." The following passage is his account of how he helped her die.

I spent a good many hours of each day sitting with her, sometimes saying nothing, sometimes speaking. When I spoke it was always, first of all, to give suggestions about her physical wellbeing. . . . I would

suggest that she was ... comfortable, free from
pain. ... These suggestions were, I think effective;
at any rate there was little pain and it was only
during the last thirty-six hours that sedation became
necessary.

... Under hypnosis M. had had, in the past, many
remarkable visionary experiences. ... She had also
had, especially while we were living in the Mojave
Desert ... a number of genuinely mystical experiences, had lived with an abiding sense of divine
immanence, of Reality totally present, moment by
moment in every object, person and event. This was
the reason for her passionate love of the desert. For
her, it was not merely a geographical region, it was
also a state of mind, a metaphysical reality, an un-
equivocal manifestation of God.

In the desert and later, under hypnosis, all M's visionary and mystical experiences had been associated
with light. (In this she was no way exceptional. Almost all mystics and visionaries have experienced
Reality in terms of light — either of light in its naked
purity, or of light infusing and radiating out of things
and persons seen with the inner eyes or in the world.)
Light had been the element in which her spirit had
lived, and it was therefore to light that all my words
referred. I would begin by reminding her of the desert she had loved so much, of the vast crystalline
silence, of the overreaching sky, of the snow-covered
mountains at whose feet we had lived. I would ask
her to open the eyes of memory to the desert sky and
to think of it as blue light of Peace, soft and yet intense, gentle and yet irresistible in its tranquilizing
power. And now, I would say, it was evening in the
desert, and the sun was setting. Overhead the sky

was more deeply blue than ever. But in the West there was a great golden illumination deepening to red; and this was the golden light of Joy, the rosy light of Love. And to the South rose the mountains, covered with snow and glowing with the white light of pure Being — the white light which is the source of the coloured lights, the absolute Being of which love, joy and peace are manifestations and to which all the dualisms of our experience, all the pairs of opposites — positive and negative, good and evil, pleasure and pain, health and sickness, life and death — are reconciled and made one. And I would ask her to look at these lights of her beloved desert and to realize that they were not merely symbols, but actual expressions of the divine nature — an expression of pure Being; an expression of the love which is at the heart of things, at the core, along with peace and joy and being, of every human mind. And having reminded her of these truths — truths which we all know in the unconscious depths of our being, which some know consciously but only theoretically and which a few (M was one of them) had known directly, albeit briefly and by snatches — I would urge her to advance into those lights, to open herself up to joy, peace, love and being, to permit herself to be irradiated by them and to become one with them. I urged her to become what in fact she had always been, what all of us have always been, a part of the divine substance, a manifestation of love, joy, and peace, a being identical with the One Reality. And I kept on repeating this, urging her to go deeper and deeper into the light, ever deeper and deeper.

So the days passed, and as her body weakened, her surface mind drifted further and further out of contact, so that she no longer recognized us or paid attention. And yet she still must have heard and understood what was said; for she would respond by appropriate action when the nurse asked her to open her mouth or swallow. . . . Addressing the deep mind which never sleeps, I went on suggesting that there should be relaxation on the physical level, and an absence of pain and nausea; and I continued to remind her of who she really was — a manifestation in time of the eternal, a part forever unseparated from the whole, of the divine reality; I went on urging her to go forward into the light.

At a little before three on Saturday morning the night nurse came and told us that the pulse was failing. I went and sat by M's bed and, from time to time, leaned over and spoke into her ear. I told her that I was with her and would always be with her in that light which was the central reality of our beings. I told her that she was surrounded by human love and that this love was the manifestation of a greater love, by which she was enveloped and sustained. I told her to let go, to forget the body, to leave it lying here like a bundle of old clothes, and to allow herself to be carried, as a child is carried, into the heart of the rosy light of love as few human beings are capable. Now she must go forward into love, must permit herself to be carried into love, deeper and deeper into it, so that at last she would be capable of loving as God loves — of loving everything, infinitely, without judging, without condemning, without either craving or abhorring. And then there was peace. How passionately, from the depth of a fatigue which illness and a frail constitution had often intensified to the point of being hardly bearable, she had longed for peace! And now she would have peace. And where there was peace and love, there too would be joy and the river of the coloured lights was carrying her towards the white light of pure being, which is the source of all things and the reconciliation of all opposites in unity. And she was to forget, not only her poor body, but the time in which that body had lived. Let her forget the past, leave her old memories behind. Regrets, nostalgias, remorses, apprehensions — all these were barriers between her and the light. Let her forget them, forget them completely, and stand here, transparent, in the presence of the light — absorbing it, allowing herself to be made one with it in the timeless now of the present instant. "Peace now," I kept repeating. "Peace, love, joy now. Being now."

For the last hour I sat or stood with my left hand on her head and the right on the solar plexus. Between two right-handed persons this contact seems to create a kind of vital circuit. For a restless child, for a sick or tired adult, there seems to be something soothing and refreshing about being in such a circuit. And so it proved even in this extremity. The breathing became quieter, and I had the impression that there was some kind of release. I went on with my suggestions and reminders, reducing them to their simplest form and repeating them close to her ear. "Let go, let go. Forget the body. Leave it lying here; it is of no importance now. Go forward into the light. Let yourself be carried into the light. No memories, no regrets, no looking backwards, no apprehensive thoughts about your own or anyone else's future. Only the light. Only this pure being, this love, this joy. Above all this peace. Peace in this timeless moment, peace now, peace now." When the breathing ceased, at about six, it was without any struggle.

Their son, Matthew, was present during those last hours, and afterward wrote his wife:

> Those last three hours were the most anguishing and moving hours of my life. . . . Aldous was whispering to her all during the time. Whispering the lesson of the *Bardo Thodol* . . . but framed in such a moving and personal way — illustrations from their lives together and incidences . . . and her own revelation of what the *Tibetan Book of the Dead* speaks about. "Let go, let go. . . ."
>
> It was over so quietly and gently with Aldous with tears streaming down his face with his quiet voice not breaking. . . .

Maria's total love for Aldous was met by his total love, enabling him to put aside his own grief and loss, to be her dragoman for the passage into the eternal season.

Eight years after Maria's passing, a few hours after John Kennedy was assassinated in Dallas, Aldous Huxley died. His own last days were spent dictating an essay on "Shakespeare and Religion." On Wednesday, November 20, he dictated the final paragraphs, beginning with Prospero's speech from *The Tempest:*

> Our revels are now ended [*sic*]. . . .
> . . . We are such stuff
> As dreams are made on, and our little life
> Is rounded with a sleep.

Prospero is here enunciating the doctrine of Maya. The world is an illusion, but is an illusion which we must take seriously, because it is as real as far as it goes, and in those aspects of the reality which we are capable of apprehending. Our business is to wake up. We have to find ways in which to detect the whole of the reality in the one illusory part which our self-centered consciousness permits us to see. We must not live thoughtlessly, taking our illusion for the complete reality, but at the same time we must not live too thoughtfully in the sense of trying to escape from the dream state. We must continually be on our watch for ways in which to enlarge our consciousness. We must not attempt to live outside the world, which is given us, but we must somehow learn how to transform it and transfigure it. Too much "wisdom" is as bad as too little wisdom, and there must be no magic tricks. We must learn how to come to reality without the enchanter's wand and his book of the words. One must find a way of being in the world while not being part of it. One must find a way of living in time without being completely swallowed up in time.

> But thought's the slave of life, and life time's fool;
> And time, that takes survey of all the world,
> Must have a stop."

On the morning of November 22, Huxley grew perceptibly weaker. Around noon, he asked for the writing tablet and scribbled a request for "100 mm" of LSD. Laura, his second wife, administered it and began talking to him, as he had to Maria, telling him to "let go, let go with ease." At five-twenty, he died.

In 1951, Cyril Connolly, a man not given to romanticizing life, had written of Huxley: "What is almost peculiar to him is the radiance of serenity and loving-kindness on his features; one no longer feels 'what a clever man' but 'what a good man,' a man at peace with himself. . . ."

Can there be a greater summation of a life?

Thomas Merton
(1915–1968)

❖❖❖

> *The monk is a bird who flies very fast*
> *without knowing where he is going. And*
> *always arrives where he went, in peace,*
> *without knowing where he comes from.*
> THOMAS MERTON
> As quoted in Monica Furlong,
> *Merton: A Biography*

None of us know our own life.

Yes, there are some who dare to know and render the life of another. We read these renderings as if we are participating in the life rendered. Why are we not satisfied with the published works, the paintings, poems, or music the subject offered to us? Was not his or her life in those? Why do we want, even demand to know more, to know what he or she was "really like"? We would shudder and die in a spasm of revulsion if we knew what we were "really like."

Since the death of Thomas Merton in 1968, books about his life and work have proliferated like dandelion fluff. I'm surprised that the networks haven't put on a miniseries called "Monk," starring Richard Chamberlain as Merton, Charles Bronson as Dom James Fox, and Jill Clayburgh as the nurse with whom Merton "fell in love." Merton's story has a little bit of everything.

Born in France and raised in England and America, Merton was an orphan by midadolescence. He fathered a child out of wedlock (the child and mother were killed in the bombing of London during the war), returned to America, and attended Columbia University, where he was known as a good man to have at a party.

Almost suddenly, however, he gave up smoking, drinking, and women. He converted to Catholicism and, after a long period of intense self-questioning, became a Trappist monk at the Abbey of Gethsemani in Kentucky, which, at the time, was as ascetic and demanding as any monastery of the Middle Ages. He became a priest and wrote an autobiography, *The Seven-Storey Mountain*. Much to his publisher's surprise, the book was a bestseller without publicity or reviews.

Merton had gone to the monastery seeking to be hidden in God. Instead, he became world-famous. He continued to write — poetry; journals; essays on literature, race relations, the nuclear-arms race; books of meditation; books on Zen Buddhism and mysticism. He became a thorn in the side of Catholic authorities who did not know what to do with this monk-celebrity. He waged an ongoing war with his abbot for permission to attend conferences and travel. But the world came to the abbey to talk with the monk-celebrity, and Merton, extroverted and exuberant, met with the hippies and the intellectuals, the theologians and scholars, and carried on a voluminous correspondence with people all over the world.

The monk-celebrity enjoyed his fame, flailed against the Catholic hierarchy that censored his manuscripts and sometimes prevented their publication, and became dissatisfied with the restrictions of monastic life (some friends got the impression that he wanted to leave it). At the same time, he campaigned successfully for permission to live as a hermit on monastery grounds.

As hermits went, he was not exactly a model; he continued to receive visitors, and it was not unknown for him to sneak over the monastery wall in search of a cold beer and a plate of fried chicken. Finally, he was permitted to travel to Asia, where he was accidentally electrocuted in his hotel room on the twenty-eighth anniversary of his entrance into the monastery.

It would make quite a movie, but it would have nothing to do with Merton. The same can be said of the official biography of Merton, *The Seven Mountains of Thomas Merton* by Michael Mott.

If one needs the facts of Merton's life, *Seven Mountains* will more than suffice. However, the facts of all our lives are the same: We are born, we fall in love (with someone and/or something), we have children (actual and/or symbolic), we suffer crises and traumas, which we endure, are wounded or destroyed by, or overcome, and one day, when we least expect it, we die, not really sure what our lives have been about and wishing we could have a little more time to find out. These are the facts of our lives. Whether they are enacted in a monastery or a suburb is just local color.

A life is a mystery, the most profound one there is. Anyone who has given birth or witnessed a birth or death is pinioned to a profound silence wherein he or she is humbled by the mystery. From whence came this life so newly born? Whence goes that life that was here an instant ago?

What is sinful is how wholly we lose the sense of mystery about life in the years between. If a biographer is to be worthy of his or her subject, he or she must not only bring this sense of mystery to the life being described and explored, he or she must write from the place of mystery and awe within. In other words, the biographer must be a contemplative, whether he or she knows it. As Merton put it in a letter to Daniel Berrigan (February 23, 1964):

God writes straight on crooked lines anyway, all the time, all the time. . . . And we I suppose are what He is writing with, though we can't see what is being written. And what He writes is not for peace of soul, that is sure.

Seven Mountains is devoid of any sense that we are what God "is writing with." Thus, Merton is absent from the pages of his biography. Mott writes as if he is not sure he likes Merton. Or, perhaps Mott's attempts at objectivity cause him to be critical so he won't be accused of hagiography. The result is silly, sometimes, as when Mott writes about Merton as the monastery's master of scholastics:

And he could be funny, very funny, though he liked to set the jokes. When one of the students started humming "Begin the Beguine" in a lecture on the Beguines, he stopped this.

As a teacher himself, Mott should know that there can be an infinite number of reasons why one will not allow certain things in the classroom. Perhaps the humming student was always attempting to be class clown. Perhaps what Merton had to say that morning was so important that he didn't want the class to begin with laughter. To claim that Merton stifled humor in the classroom merely because "he liked to set the jokes" does not follow from the example.

The profound and impossible challenge of biography is to render a life both as its subject experienced it and as those around him experienced it. Mott's failure is that he seems more interested in Merton the writer than Merton the monk. Though Mott tries, the biography gives no feeling for what the contemplative life is and how Merton lived it, what his struggles were with it and within it. Mott is very good at portraying the public Merton, particularly his role in and disagreements with the antinuclear movement in the early sixties and the anti–Vietnam War movement later in the decade. But Mott has no sense of the inner Merton, which is disappointing, since he had access to restricted materials.

The most controversial part of the book is the "revelation" of Merton's intense, nonsexual love relationship with a nurse he met while hospitalized in Louisville, Kentucky. There is something charming in the story of this middle-aged monk acting like an adolescent boy. There is even courage in the fact that Merton, a monk, would allow himself such feelings, such pain, such struggle, and such joy.

The relationship was not secret, either within the monastery or to Merton's close friends outside. But because Mott fails to give us a sense of the meaning and impact of the relationship on Merton's inner life, we are left with gossip instead of story-as-revelation.

Mott's biography is as sober and dull as an English-department faculty meeting. Merton was neither. His being was far more akin to van Gogh's *Starry Night* — anarchic, exuberant, bursting with vitality, energy, and fun.

2 ✧✧✧

> *But what is life but uncertainties and a few plausible possibilities?*
> THOMAS MERTON

More modest in size is Monica Furlong's *Merton: A Biography*. It is also superior to Mott's. Focused on Merton's life as a monk and contemplative, Furlong chooses the far more difficult nuances of the soul's ever-changing colors for rendering her portrait.

For example, Merton was frequently ill and was hospitalized many times for operations. Where Mott gives the details of his hospital stays and his illnesses, Furlong links his illnesses and operations to his spiritual life:

> Dom Eudes Bamberger has described Merton as having four times the psychic energy of most ordinary men but suggests that his psychic energy exhausted his physical frame. . . . It may have been just this awareness of a tendency to live with a destructive vigor that drove him first to the relative seclusion of Gethsemani, and then to the further seclusion (imperfect as it was) of the hermit life, but even so his body paid a heavy price for the adventures of his mind and spirit. From the early 1960s onward, he suffered from a series of minor and major complaints, some of which caused him considerable distress.

Furlong is also quite good in describing Merton's life as a contemplative, especially his years in the hermitage. She not only describes his daily routine there, but also, using Merton's words, provides the reader with the sounds and sights of life in the hermitage through the seasons.

One of the most remarkable facts about Merton is that he had only two hours a day in which to write. How he was able to write not only as much as he did but as well is almost beyond comprehension. Furlong is able to bring us close to understanding. By her descriptions of the contemplative life, we sense that one of its fruits for Merton was an increased ability to concentrate and to focus his energies wholly and completely on whatever task was before him. Thus, the act of writing became an act of contemplation, another dimension of prayer. As Merton remarked:

Such writing as I do (when I work I manage to write quickly) is not any part of a career, nor do I even conceive of it as an apostolate. It is simply a way of meditating on paper. If others wish to share in it, they are welcome, because I too have no proprietorship over these thoughts which are not "mine" and which if they are given are not given just to "me." (Letter to Dona Louisa Coomaraswamy, January 13, 1961)

There was a difference between the act of writing and being known as a writer. In *The Sign of Jonas*, Merton wrote:

An author in a Trappist monastery is like a duck in a chicken coop. And he would give anything in the world to be a chicken instead of a duck.

Being an author is a public role. Merton wrote from inner necessity; and given not only the quantity of his published material but the journals and thousands of letters he wrote, one might say that he was compelled to write.

If the monastic life is a life of hardship and sacrifice, I would say that for me most of the hardship has come in connection with writing. It is possible to doubt whether I have become a monk (a doubt I have to live with), but it is not possible to doubt that I am a writer, that I was born one and will die as one. Disconcerting, disedifying as it is, this seems to be my lot and my vocation. . . . I have also had to accept the fact that my life is almost totally paradoxical. I have also had to learn gradually to get along without apologizing for the fact, even to myself. . . . It is in the paradox itself, the paradox which was and still is a source of insecurity, that I have come to find the greatest security. I have become convinced that the very contradictions in my life are in some ways signs of God's mercy to me: if only because someone so complicated and so prone to confusion and self-defeat could hardly survive for long without special mercy. (Quoted in Furlong, *Merton*)

While Furlong comes closer to seeing the contemplative and writer in Merton as belonging to a whole, she shares with Mott a failure to see how Merton's relationship with Dom James Fox, the abbot, belongs to the whole, also. Since Merton's death, Dom James has been portrayed as the primary nemesis of Merton's life. Merton is partially responsible for this. That it was a stormy and difficult relationship cannot be questioned. As abbot, it was Dom James who repeatedly refused Merton's requests to travel to conferences, to transfer to another monastic order, and to be a hermit. Merton vented his frustration and anger in letters to friends and in person when they visited. He gave the impression that Dom James viewed him as Gethsemani's prize commodity, like the cheese and fruitcake for which the monastery was famous, and that the abbot felt Merton might never return to the monastery if he were allowed to travel, which would not look good for Gethsemani or the church.

Yet, if the relationship between Merton and Dom James was as bad as both Mott and Furlong maintain, why was Merton chosen, first, to be master of scholastics, the third-highest position in the monastery's hierarchy, and, later, novice master, a position second in importance only to that of the abbot. The abbot who appointed him novice master was none other than Dom James.

As novice master, Merton was responsible for the education of those wanting to become fully vowed monks. If

Dom James was as antagonistic to Merton as Mott, Furlong, and others would have us believe, why did he entrust the novices to him? Neither biographer mentions, either, that for the last fifteen years of his life, Merton was Dom James's confessor.

It is surprising and disappointing that neither writer quotes from Dom James's very moving account of his relationship with Merton, "The Spiritual Son," published in *Thomas Merton, Monk: A Monastic Tribute.* (Edited by Brother Patrick Hart, Merton's secretary, the volume appeared in 1974 and is a collection of essays by fellow monks about Merton; together with the Furlong biography, it provides a full and very human portrait of Merton.) Because so much has been written and whispered about the relationship with Dom James and about its adverse effect on Merton, it is worth quoting extensively from the abbot's essay, as it reveals much that both biographies chose to ignore.

One of Merton's joys was taking walks in the woods outside the abbey's enclosure. Once, during a visit to the monastery, the order's superiors from France mandated that such walks were not appropriate for cloistered monks. Merton, known as Father Louis within the order, was acting as translator when the edict was handed down. Dom James recalled:

> I looked at Fr. Louis. His face flushed red and big tears filled his eyes. He quivered a bit, but never said a word. He remained silent, seemingly crushed. To think that that one "exercise" which he loved so much, and legitimately, was to be denied him! Many thoughts ran through my mind, but I concluded that there was no need arguing then.

Dom James simply appointed Merton to the theretofore nonexistent position of "Chief Ranger of the Forests," whose duties were to mark the trees to be cut for firewood and carpentry work and to keep the forests cleared of fallen trees.

Sometime later, the state forestry department was given permission to erect a tall fire tower on monastery property. The tower was made of steel and had a large cabin at the very top in which the fire warden would live while watching for forest fires. Merton proposed to Dom James that he be considered for the job of fire warden, because the tower was ideal for a hermitage.

Dom James agreed and said that he would seek permission from the head of the order in France. Permission was granted, but on one condition: Merton would have to be fully a hermit, with absolutely no contacts with the monastic community. The news was conveyed to Merton. Three days later, he came to Dom James and volunteered for the recently vacated position of novice master.

Though in his correspondence Merton presents only the negative side of his relationship with Dom James, the abbot observes that "during the twenty years we lived together, he never missed a week in coming over to the office to converse with me." Dom James writes further that

> sometimes during Confession, our conversation would wander to extrinsic problems. Some five or ten minutes would pass, without either of us being aware of it. Suddenly he would cry out: "Hey, Reverend Father, let me give you Absolution, and get you off your knees."
>
> To which I would reply, "O.K., but first soak me with a good penance for being such a tough old Superior." He never would.

The most moving part of Dom James's essay is a letter he wrote Merton while the latter was on his Asian journey.

Dom James writes eloquently of his own desire to be a hermit and how many times his superiors had refused him.

> My first reaction was to lean toward harsh and un-charitable thoughts in their regard, and even to question their motivations. But how wrong I would have been. Indeed to all outward appearances, it seemed that they were unjust and narrow. But looking through and beyond and above the appearances, they were merely instruments whom God was using to convey His will to me — at that time. . . .
>
> . . . I would not be in the least surprised if at times I have indeed appeared as your "public enemy No. 1" — your "bête noire" — your haunting "Nemesis." But in reality, I am not so.
>
> You never had — nor will you ever have — one who has been a more faithful and loyal friend and brother than myself. I never had any other motive in any decisions in your regard than your best — not necessarily your best temporal interests — but your best eternal interests. As Psalm 76 phrases it: "And I had in mind the Eternal Years."
>
> . . . in regard to your present trip to the Orient which you desired for several years, and for which you did not receive permission, I was only an instrument in God's hands. God's time for it had not come.
>
> Now His time has come. . . .

That Dom James needed to write such a letter certainly indicates that his relationship with Merton was not an easy one. What is also clear, however, is the abbot's deep need to know that he and Merton were reconciled, despite it all. This is especially poignant because, at the time the letter was written, Dom James had ceased to be abbot and was living as a hermit, something about which he had sought and received Merton's counsel and advice.

Merton wrote back from Calcutta:

I have been waiting for a chance to thank you for your warm and gracious letter. I want you to know that I appreciate it. Certainly you must not feel that I failed to understand the situation.

Personally, I never resented any of your decisions, because I knew you were following your conscience and the policies that seemed necessary then.

... Be sure, that I have never changed in my respect for you as Abbot, and affection as Father. Our different views certainly did not affect our deep agreement on the real point of life and of our vocation.

Even a cursory perusal of Merton's letters makes one question his saying that he "never resented" Dom James's decisions regarding him. The resentment and anger are strongly expressed in the letters. Yet, in these letters one can also hear Merton, the orphaned adolescent, reaching out for sympathy, approval, and acceptance, presenting his case as one-sidedly as possible in order to receive in return the mother's love the little boy in him still needed and craved. In that context, his letter to Dom James can be seen as sincere. What the ego may resent and be angered by, the soul receives gladly. Like any of us, Merton spoke both from the ego and the soul. In his final letter to James Fox, Merton would appear to be writing from the soul.

Despite Monica Furlong's unsympathetic treatment of the Fox-Merton relationship, her biography understands Merton the contemplative. Her choice of what to quote from Merton is always sure and illuminating. She does not overemphasize Merton the social and political thinker as Mott does. Neither does she seek to explain what she does not understand. She respects a mystery and because she does, she takes us close to the mystery of who this man Merton was.

3 ✧✧✧

The best my friendship can offer you is
prayer, during the psalms at night, in my
Mass at dawn. (I have a rare privilege,
unappreciated and unthought of by almost
all priests even here, of saying Mass just at
sunrise, when the light of the sun falls on
the altar, and powerfully lights up the
mystery of the divine presence spoken of in
so many, many prayers of illumination, like
this morning's postcommunion: "Come to
meet us always O Lord with the heavenly
Light everywhere, that we may discern
with clear mind the mystery of which you
have made us partakers, and that we may
enter into it with awe and love."
LETTER FROM THOMAS MERTON TO
DONA LUISA COOMARASWAMY
January 13, 1961

There are some thirty-five hundred letters of Mer-
ton's — written to more than a thousand people — at the
Thomas Merton Studies Center in Bellarmine College in
Louisville. *The Hidden Ground of Love: The Letters of*
Thomas Merton on Religious Experience and Social Con-
cerns is the first published volume of these letters.

Selected and edited by William Shannon, the collection
is unsatisfying for reasons that probably cannot be helped.
Arranging the volume by subject matter has made the
reading slow and tedious sometimes. Regardless of how
noble it is to be opposed to nuclear weapons, letter after
letter on the subject can be tiring. After one has said he's
"agin" it, there really isn't much more to be said.

The editor has also chosen to arrange the volume
chronologically by correspondent rather than in straight

chronology. There might have been an advantage in seeing the correspondence to, for example, Dorothy Day, in chronological order if Merton's relationship to Day or any of his correspondents had changed in some substantial way. Because his relationships did not, this means of organizing the letters has little merit.

One cannot but be overwhelmed by the scope of Merton's mind as revealed in these letters, however. Among the people written to are Thich Nhat Hanh, W. H. Ferry, Erich Fromm, Abraham Joshua Heschel, Zalman Schacter, Aldous Huxley, Daniel Berrigan, Dom Helder Camara, Dorothy Day, James Douglass, James Forest, Gordon Zahn, Rosemary Reuther, Paul Tillich, Martin E. Marty, Corrett King, two popes, Jacqueline and Ethel Kennedy, Lyndon Johnson, and D. T. Suzuki. Subjects discussed with astounding knowledge and in detail include Zen Buddhism, Hinduism, Judaism, Sufism, race, Catholicism, Protestanism, Christianity, and pacifism.

What becomes apparent in the letters is that there were many people living behind the names Thomas Merton/ Father Louis. He is deferential and polite when writing to Orientals, courteous and respectful to Dorothy Day, argumentative and needy to Rosemary Reuther, and downright obsequious to church superiors. The intellectual content of the letters is quite high, so much so that the personal voice that speaks in the journals appears infrequently. Yet, the letters are studded with the simplicity and insight that characterize Merton's published work.

> . . . the law of all spiritual life is the law of risk and struggle, and possible failure. (To Edward Deming Andrews, September 20, 1962)

> Some of us only learn tolerance and understanding after having been intolerant and "absolute." In a

word, it is hard to live with a strict and sometimes absurd ideal, and the ambivalence involved can be tragic, or salutary. (Ibid.)

That is all I do. Throw stones in the air, and if somebody yells I know the stones came down. (To Daniel Berrigan, February 23, 1964)

The Lord has been very good and yet I still fight my way through the forests. This is to be expected. (To Sister M. Emmanuel, July 28, 1960)

It is so strange to advance backwards and to get where you are going in a totally unexpected way. (Ibid.)

J. was also horrifying me with tales of the sedate gambling places at Lake Tahoe, the ones that are prim and country-clubbish and which cater to decent people, with dealerettes in prim black dresses, and soft Muzak, and nary a drunk on the premises, and the nice old ladies coming up to gamble in busloads from the cities of the plain. I am utterly disheartened. What has happened to good old sin? Here I am behind these walls doing my bit and counting on the world to do its bit, with barrelhouse piano and the walleyed guys in shades, with long cigars, raking in the pieces of eight, and the incandescent floozies lolling over the roulette wheels. . . . Tell me, Ping, am I wasting my time? Is all that utterly gone? I am shaken. How can I go into a week's retreat if all has . . . GONE? But maybe there is still plenty of evil in other fields. I take heart again and get back to the sackcloth. (To W. H. Ferry, January 18, 1962)

Why not cry out to God in any way you like, as long as you don't expect it to console you. (To Etta Gullick, August 31, 1962)

... pray as the Spirit moves you, but of course I would say follow the Mass in a missal unless there is a good reason for doing something else, like floating suspended ten feet above the congregation. (To John Harris, June 22, 1959)

... the anguish must always be there. But it must deepen and change and become vastly more fruitful. That is the best we can hope for nowadays: a fruitful anguish instead of one that is utterly sterile and consuming. (Idem, September 12, 1959)

The concrete existential situation you are in here and now, whatever it is, contains for you God's will, reality. Your only job is to accept it as it is, because it is His will, and seek to fulfill it because it is the truth, not because it pleases you, gets you off a hook, or on a hook, or makes you feel safe, or whatever. But in order to do this you have to really believe deeply in God's love for you, and see that even the "evil" in your life can serve the purpose of His love, now that it is over and the effects have to be suffered. . . . you may have a great deal to suffer, but if you accept it realistically and without too much fear, with real trust in Him, it will do great things for you. But it may be painful and confusing. . . . (To Linda Parsons Sabbath, January 29, 1966)

Reading the letters, one encounters the many faces of Merton directly. Given how prolific a writer he was, why are his own words not sufficient to tell us who this man was? Why is it that what a person offers publicly of his or her life no longer satisfies us? Are we rapidly losing all sense of the private, the personal, the mysterious? Do we no longer know that there is a realm of the individual that is the province of that person and God? Do we really think we can truly know another human being? The further we live from the awe and mystery of our lives, the more intense the need to deprive the lives of others of awe and mystery.

4 ✧✧✧

> *. . . one of the marks of the authentic*
> *contemplative is a growing need to hide*
> *himself, to draw ever more deeply into*
> *secrecy, to efface himself, become invisible.*
> JOHN HOWARD GRIFFIN,
> *The Hermitage Journals*

On September 9, 1980, John Howard Griffin died of complications from diabetes, in Fort Worth, Texas. He had been chosen to write the official biography of Thomas Merton. Though he began, increasing ill health prevented his ever working on it extensively.

Most remember Griffin as the white man who "dyed" his skin and traveled through the South for six weeks in 1959 because he wanted to know what it was like to be black in America. The subsequent book describing his journey, *Black Like Me*, became a bestseller. It will be a travesty if he is remembered for that book only.

Born in Dallas in 1920, Griffin was educated to be a doctor, and was a recognized authority on Gregorian chants by the time he was twenty-one. He worked in the French underground in World War II and helped smuggle Jews out of Nazi Germany. Forced finally to flee Europe or risk capture, he enlisted and was sent to the South Pacific, where an exploding bomb left him blind in 1946. He did not regain his sight until 1957, when he saw his wife and children for the first time.

During the years of his blindness, he wrote two novels — *The Devil Rides Outside* and *Nuni*. No summary of their plots and themes can do justice to their richness and depth. Both are serious and complex works. "Nothing like them has been written in American fiction of the modern period," wrote critic Maxwell Geismar. "For sheer talent, power and virtuosity of craft, Griffin ranks very high." Unfortunately, both novels have been long out of print, and while excerpts were published in *The John Howard Griffin Reader,* edited by Bradford Daniel, it, too, is out of print.

It is significant that Griffin's novelistic output is limited to the years of his blindness. He had many novels in progress, but as much as he loved writing, Griffin was not a literary man. Besides *Black Like Me,* only two other books of his were published: *Land of the High Sky,* a short historical work about the Staked Plain area of Texas, and *A Hidden Wholeness,* which features the photographs of Thomas Merton.

The latter book may give a clue as to why Griffin did not fulfill himself as a novelist: he chose to fulfill himself as a human being. *A Hidden Wholeness* is as close as one can come to holding a Bach cantata in one's hands. It features Griffin's text, some photographs of his, and mainly those of Merton, taken primarily at the Abbey of Gethsemani. The book is supposed to be about Merton, but it is really a commingling of Merton's spirit and Griffin's. The two were close friends, even spiritual brothers; each lived out a part of life the other chose not to.

Merton was the contemplative in the cloister; Griffin was the contemplative in the world — husband, father, social activist, journalist. What characterizes the work and lives of both men is contemplation as the "gift of awareness, an awakening to the Real within all that is real" (Merton, *New Seeds of Contemplation*). Merton also described contemplation as "life itself, fully awake, fully active, fully aware that it is alive. It is spiritual wonder. It is gratitude for life, for awareness and for being" (ibid.).

This contemplative core in Griffin is heard also in his other works: "Nowadays we seek happiness and we seek love; in my day we believed we had to be happiness and love," he wrote in *The Devil Rides Outside*. In a 1959 letter to his friend Decherd Turner, he wrote about writing and also about himself: "The writing is basically nothing more than the overflow of this great love which causes men to throw out all the paraphernalia of what is in favor of what ought to be" (as quoted in *The John Howard Griffin Reader*).

It was this abiding sense of "what ought to be" that compelled Griffin to become a black man. It is this same sense that pervades his posthumous books *The Hermitage Journals: A Diary Kept While Working on the Biography of Thomas Merton* and *Follow the Ecstasy: Thomas Merton, The Hermitage Years, 1965–1968,* both published in 1983. The latter represents what of the Merton biography Griffin was able to complete, and is more than ample confirmation that he was the only one who could have rendered Merton's life as an act of contemplation.

Using Merton's unpublished journals as the basis for his narration, Griffin employs a technique that is more novelistic than conventionally biographical. Through Griffin's adept paraphrasing and quoting from the journals, the reader lives in the hermitage with/as Merton. This is a radical departure for biography, a genre in which the biographer usually places him/herself between the reader and the subject and acts as interpreter and guide. Griffin does just the opposite: he removes himself, and even when he becomes part of the narrative, he mentions himself in the third person.

Because of Griffin's attention to the detail of Merton's routine at the hermitage, the reader begins to taste the various qualities of solitude as seen in deer tracks in the snow, or heard in falling trees during an electrical storm. The reader feels the pain of Merton's bursitis, the malady that sometimes made it impossible for him to type or even write by hand. It is a simple story Griffin attempts to tell, a story with no drama except that of a monk learning to be a hermit because that is how he has been called to love God. Thus, it is a story of dailiness, a story of recording what was eaten for breakfast, and of how hard the brightness of the stars is on a winter night and how enervating the heat of a summer day is. Because Griffin chose to seek the inner Merton through a careful rendering of dailiness, the inner Merton is revealed with a power the more conventional biographies cannot approximate.

Especially sensitive is Griffin's handling of Merton's relationship with the nurse. Using the unpublished journals, Merton's ecstasy and agony are experienced by the reader so that the story is removed from the level of gossip and becomes a story of revelation in which Merton learns how full his capacity to love is — something that he had always doubted. This doubt had made him question his capacity to love God. Through his love for the nurse, and especially the agonizing rejection of that love's consummation, the life of Merton the monk was deepened by the brave foolishness of Merton the man.

Also worth noting is how much warmer Merton's relationship with Dom James is as portrayed in *Follow the Ecstasy*. Griffin allows Merton to speak for himself, and in the quotes and paraphrases from the unpublished journals, one sees clearly how much Merton not only needed but used Dom James to protect him from the world as well as his own weaknesses. Particularly moving is the sensitivity and caring with which Dom James handled Merton's relationship with the nurse.

Griffin's approach to the life of Merton succeeds only because Griffin risked himself. Where other biographers went to the libraries to read Merton's letters and manuscripts, where other biographers went to France to see the house in which Merton was born, Griffin went to live at Merton's hermitage.

The Hermitage Journals has more to say about Griffin than Merton. That is as it should be. Merton's life as a contemplative can have meaning for us only to the extent that Merton does not become an end in himself, a New Age icon we look on and say, "Oh, wow!" If the life of Merton means anything, it is a call to "interior intimacy . . . that kind of intimacy that melts all the crusts within one" (*The Hermitage Journals*).

Griffin's journals speak with the same tones of authenticity as Merton's, not because Griffin is attempting to write like Merton, but because Griffin writes from the place of oneness wherein all is and ever will be.

> Words are like rubber balls that a man tries to throw up to the clouds. They will not reach. To be moderate in matters of love is simply not to love. To be moderate in matters of justice is to be simply unjust.

> Blemishes are for people who do not know about love. We hide our blemishes or minimize them for people who do not know about love.

Above all, Griffin loves that mystery which was his life, which was Merton's life.

> Only after his [Merton's] death did many of his friends know a great deal about him. His hidden life

was quite deeply private and hidden. No one, not even those who were very close to him, really knew his "secret prayer." He revealed those facts of himself that were proper to each of his friends: but underneath this was his vocation as monk and hermit — something between himself and God alone, something that had to remain secret because these things become distorted when known.

Perhaps that is my unease with the books being written about Merton and his work. I do not fear damage to Merton. It is the damage to ourselves that terrifies me.

We have not sat in our own hermitages and therefore we no longer know that there are, indeed, some things that must remain secret. We no longer know that there are those things that are secret between ourselves and God. Even more, there are those things that are secret only to God.

Nothing belongs more to God than the secret of who another is.

To Be a Writer
and Be Black

✧✧✧

When I was twenty-one, I wanted to move to New Hampshire and live haiku. Haiku is more than the three-line, seventeen-syllable poems elementary-school teachers think are appropriate for children. Haiku is a spiritual discipline, a way of Being out of which one writes deceptively simple poems that burst with silence and peel back the layers of perception until the All and Nothingness that is all and evermore is revealed.

That was the life to which I wanted to give myself. I got as close to New Hampshire as western Massachusetts, but I haven't written a haiku in more years than I can recall.

Another reality impinged on my life like an eternal winter of burning winds and snows so white and dazzling that the eyes could find comfort only in blindness. Instead of living and writing haiku, I became a voice of the black collective and wrote books and essays articulating the pain, suffering, and rage of blacks.

Then, one spring afternoon in the early seventies, I learned that the black collective cared only for itself, and its ultimate triumph would be to destroy that singular entity I knew as myself.

60

I spoke at a high school in Harlem. During the question-and-answer period I was asked: "What should black people do?" The question was repeated with that desperate sincerity which belongs to adolescence.

It was a good question. Richard Nixon was president. The sixties were over and white people were tired of social change. Most of the liberal social programs had been dismantled and the message to blacks was, you are on your own. So what blacks should do was a cogent question.

"I don't know. What do you think we should do?" I answered the question in its many guises.

My refusal to say more seemed to anger them. Finally, someone yelled, "We demand that you lead us!"

I refused the dubious honor.

"Then what good are you?" someone else yelled.

"Absolutely none!" I shot back.

My responsibilities as a black writer did not include being a leader. That would be to sell my birthright.

I must have appeared indifferent and even arrogant in the face of their poverty and desperation, because suddenly the principal was beside me. "I'd better get you out of here." And I was hustled from the auditorium and out of the building.

If I had any response to the afternoon, it was not sympathy or empathy with the students. It was anger that as a black writer I was expected to do more than write. I was made to feel that if all I could do was write, then my words were inadequate to the problem. If I could not be what they needed me to be, they did not want me to be.

That is part of the nature of collectives. The individual is of value only as long as he or she serves the collective in the way the collective demands to be served. The collective has no interest other than itself.

Ten years later I found myself on a panel discussing racism in children's books. One of the black panelists presented examples of books she considered antiblack. When the time came for audience questions, one of the few whites present said, quietly but firmly, "I object to your calling my book racist," and mentioned the name of a book that had been criticized by the panelist.

The black panelist responded, "Your book is one of the most racist books I've ever read," and, producing a sheaf of notes, began citing page numbers and reading passages from the book. All the excerpts were highlighted by prominent use of the word *nigger* and disparaging remarks about same. The black audience responded with mutterings of shock and disapproval. And there the matter rested.

I was not so estranged from the black collective that I did not understand the black panelist's anger. The use of *nigger* and derogatory comments about "niggers" from white characters cannot be read as if we did not live in a society where that word and those comments might not be repeated by a white child to a black one outside the classroom.

I also understood the white author's denial of racism. The book was set in the South at a time when such language and opinions were the norm. If the author was to be true to history, there was no choice but to use the language and opinions of that time and that place. As a writer I would have done the same.

The white author's context was historical; the black panelist's context was today. Was there a way to reconcile the integrity of both?

Almost by definition, the black writer is supposed to be the voice for a people whose cries are not heard, whose laughter is not shared. We are called upon to conjure words, powerful and magical, to counteract those that have flowed and continue to flow from pens held by whites, words that humiliate and disparage us — words whose impact only increases the hatreds that would kill us.

Three examples: The *New York Times Book Review* (December 14, 1980) asked novelist Joyce Carol Oates to reflect on the future of the novel. Among her provocative comments was the following: "I anticipate, in my idealism . . . novels by minorities that range beyond the passionate but delimited concerns of minorities." Who is she to define black suffering as a "delimited concern"? Are black experiences to be cavalierly dismissed because she is "delimited" in her concerns?

The second example is from a *Newsweek* review (January 5, 1981) of a movie starring Goldie Hawn: "Goldie is an incorrigible liberal who defends and brings into her house every oppressed minority: blacks, Chicanos, Indians — and stray dogs. The only ones who don't rip her off are the dogs." Am I being "delimitedly concerned" if I object to being equated with "stray dogs"?

The final example is from a survey of children's literature published in *Time* (December 29, 1980): "All is [not] dragonfree in the world of children's literature. The fragmentation of the nuclear family, the new consciousness of black and women's history and of human rights in general have engendered a series of 'problem books' that confuse as often as they enlighten." Are the sum of the achievements of Virginia Hamilton, Mildred Taylor, John Steptoe, myself, and others to be reduced to "problem books"?

The message of these three excerpts is that neither black writers nor black lives are to be considered seriously. The implication is that the only important values are those considered so by whites. Blacks and women are the dragons in the bountiful garden of children's literature. (And we all know what happens to dragons in children's books.)

Yes, we write "problem books," because we know what a problem whites have created of themselves for us. We write "problem books" because we want *all* children to be better able to grapple with the Hydra-heads of racism than we were at their age.

Hannah Arendt wrote that "it is the poet's task to coin the words we live by." Black writers are engaged in a new minting process that is not exclusive to them. Though our country is racially fragmented, the human condition is not the sole property of any group, despite the impression one might receive from books by many whites.

I wish the black panelist had said to the white writer that there is a fidelity to the human condition deeper than fidelity to the language of a particular time and place. Fidelity to the language of time and place can be a source of pain to blacks because it is part of the reality we must confront in this time and this place. And fidelity to the human condition means to love the soul and its potential for beauty and truth even as that soul seems mired in the worst of the human condition.

I imagine that the white writer would have responded, "That is just what I tried to do," pulled out a copy of the book, and read passages that proved it.

Then the black panelist could have said, "I am so afraid that the language in your book will make a white child feel confirmed in using such language and in expressing such attitudes."

"That is the risk," the white writer might've said.

"But at whose expense?"

"Yours *and* mine," would've come the response. "Yours and mine."

❖❖❖

May Sarton was asked once how she wanted to be remembered.

"As wholly human," she responded.

Only to the extent that I am wholly human do I fulfill

my responsibility as a black writer, because my responsibility is not to black people only, despite the responsibilities history may impose on a black writer, despite whatever duty one may feel to the black collective.

My responsibility as a black writer is to the ideal of the human. If that is to be the heartbeat of my writing, I cannot succumb to collective definitions and collective ways of Being. To do so is to act irresponsibly in relationship to my gift.

To be responsible as a writer means that every word of mine will have been written truly, as truly as I knew how at the time of the writing. That is only the beginning, however, because writing, though done in solitude, is a social act. It needs the reader to complete it. Writing is a relationship in which I who write and you who read meet in the silent places of your soul. If I have written well and you have read well, we learn a little more about what it means to be wholly human.

Martin Buber wrote that to read a book one "must labor with it hours at a time as with a headstrong horse, until covered with sweat he stands in front of it and reads this book he has tamed."

One who writes needs those who can read, who bring to the act of reading all the levels and nuances of not only mind but feeling that a responsible writer brings to the act of writing. To write and publish is to risk oneself in the world. It is not too much to ask that readers risk themselves when they read.

Being responsible is the act of making a promise to another. As a black writer my promise cannot be made exclusively to blacks. When asked for whom she wrote, Joyce Carol Oates responded, "God." That is my answer, too.

My promise is to that part of you which is beyond and separate from definitions of gender, race, and all the sociological and political descriptions that hang from our limbs and rattle like the chains of Marley's ghost. There is a place of sacred truth in each of us. It is from within that place I seek to write and it is to that place in you my words seek to go.

A black critic wrote of me once that "because he is black he is by virtue of these political and social conditions, a member of a racial collective. He does not have the freedom of defining himself completely outside the boundaries of race and its ramifications. . . . the highly individual nature of his quest ignores his surrounding substantive reality — that of a black man living in Twentieth-century America."

That is too simple. It is also false.

If I take responsibility for that place of sacred truth within, then I know that my "substantive reality" does not differ from that of anyone who has ever existed on the planet. Thus, what I must take responsibility for, ultimately, is the Unseen and the Unknowable.

Reb Simchah Bunam wrote:

> The Lord created the world in a state of beginning. The universe is always in an uncompleted state, in the form of its beginning. It is not like a vessel at which the master works to finish it; it requires continuous labor and renewal by creative forces. Should these cease for only a second, the universe would return to primeval chaos.

My responsibility as a black writer does not differ from my responsibility as a human being: to live with reverence toward and responsibility for my soul.

Reb Leib went to see the Maggid of Mezhirich not to hear him discuss Torah but to watch him tie his shoes.

We must learn to tie our shoes.

The Beechwood Staff

❖❖❖

I have always loved books. Medical science has learned that infants suck their thumbs in the womb. I read. I love books as much for their sheer physicality as for what I may learn and experience through the words on their pages. I love to touch books, to hold them. They are my security blanket, and whether I am happy or depressed, I go to bookstores to orient myself to the world, to feel myself enclosed, almost womblike, by books on all sides. I need books, almost as an alcoholic needs liquor. When I was in college, I always carried a book with me on dates, not sure that any girl could be as interesting or involving as a book. My wife wonders if I've changed.

The center of my house is my library, with floor-to-ceiling bookshelves holding ten thousand or so books. Sometimes, late at night, when the house is finally quiet, I sit in my big overstuffed chair and stare at the shelves and am overcome by sadness because when I die, I will miss my books. I have sworn to haunt my children eternally if they sell any of my books. But they needn't worry. I will be the first person ever buried in a grave with floor-to-ceiling bookcases.

In 1956, when I entered college, I was a chemistry major because I felt I should do something useful with my life. That aberration passed quickly when I received a D in freshman math. So I was faced with a decision: what to do with my life. The only thing I truly loved was books.

A quick perusal of the want ads convinced me that no one would pay me to stay at home and read. But reading was what I loved to do. When students ask me what they should do with their lives, I always ask, "What do you love?" And before they tell me, I add, "Follow what you love, and you'll be all right."

I loved to read, and I followed my love and became an English major. Nothing could have been more useless, but it allowed me to do what I love. I didn't read much English or American literature, however, preferring French fiction, Chinese and Japanese poetry, history, philosophy, religion, and theology. And to the D in freshman math, I added one in Neoclassical and Romantic Poetry.

My four years of reading came rapidly to an end, and the question of what to do with my life had to be faced again. I was *expertly* prepared now to make my living reading, but my highly developed skills were not in demand.

So I asked again, What do you love? The answer was more fervent now: I love books. And from that indiscriminate love came the decision to be a writer. Although the decision seemed perfectly logical then, it is obvious now that I came to be a writer through a curious back road. I became a writer not because I felt that I was particularly talented, not because there was something burning inside me that I had to tell the world, not for any of the reasons writers usually have. I became a writer because I love books, and how can one live without expressing his or her love?

This love of books is a sweet mystery to me. Why are books more real to me than most people? Why do I forget the names and faces of people but can take a book from my library shelves and remember where I was sitting when I read it, what the weather was, and what the room was like in whatever apartment or house I was then inhabiting?

I am intrigued that the word *book* comes from a Germanic root, which means "beech tree" — a reference to the beech staff on which ancient Germans carved runes. It is a haunting image of origins, this rune-inscribed beech staff standing in a forest clearing. It does not matter, really, what the runes represented. What is significant is that the staff was there, that one person was attempting to reach out to others whom he or she may not have known.

I wish I could recall the first book I read at the age of four or five, or the first book read to me by my mother. Whenever the experience began, I'm sure it was a profound one of knowing that someone I didn't know was reaching out to me across the vastness.

I grew up in the forties and fifties in Kansas City, Kansas, and Nashville, Tennessee, with summers spent in Arkansas. The forties and fifties were not pleasant times for blacks and I am offended by white people who get nostalgic for the fifties. I have no nostalgia for segregation, for the "No Colored Allowed" signs covering the landscape like litter on the smooth, green grass of a park. I have no nostalgia for a time when I endangered my life if, while downtown shopping with my parents, I raised my eyes and accidentally met the eyes of a white woman. Black men and boys were lynched for this during my childhood and adolesence. It is a world I recall with the pain of inner screaming, and I survived that world partly because I discovered the beech staff standing in the forest clearing, covered with runes.

Although I don't recall any specific content of books from my early years, there was the more important emotional content those books represented — the knowledge that the segregated world I was forced to live in was not the only reality. Somewhere beyond that world, somewhere my eyes could not then penetrate, were dreams and possibilities, and I knew this was true because the books I read ravenously, desperately, were voices from that world.

The mystery and miracle of a book is found precisely in the fact that it is a solitary voice penetrating time and space until it goes beyond time and space to alight for a moment in that place within us that is also beyond time and space. Let me explain. I am an indiscriminate reader. By accepted and respected literary standards, my taste in books can be execrable. I buy books in bus stations and drugstores as well as respectable bookshops. I have read trashy novels with as much pleasure as I have derived from acknowledged literary masterpieces. I have no shame about this because I trust that something-in-me which knows what I need and directs me to it when my more conscious self is unaware that anything may be amiss.

When I was growing up in Nashville, blacks were not permitted in the main library — a situation I rectified at the age of sixteen when I desegregated the library single-handedly. Before that, however, my primary access to books was the bookmobile that came to my neighborhood every Friday evening. Its stock of books was not only limited in number but restricted in subject matter, consisting primarily of westerns and mysteries discarded from the many white libraries in town. So, from fourteen to sixteen, I read nothing but western novels and Perry Mason mysteries. Crawling into bed at seven in the evening, I sometimes read two a night. Fortunately, my parents were so glad I was at home and not out running the streets that

they didn't care what I read. But maybe, too, they understood on some primal level what I was doing, although at
the time I did not.

I grew up in a violent world. Segregation was a deathly
spiritual violence, not only in its many restrictions on
where we could live, eat, go to school, and go after dark.
There was also the constant threat of physical death if you
looked at a white man in what he considered the wrong
way or if he didn't like your attitude. There was also the
physical violence of my community. I will forego a recital
of the deaths from stabbings and shootings and of the
classmates imprisoned for rapes that never occurred, because it is a recital almost any black person could give as
calmly as giving a weather report. What I have realized is
that on those nights I lay in bed reading westerns and detective novels, I was attempting to neutralize and withstand the violence that was so much a part of my dailiness.
In westerns and mysteries I found a kind of mirror in
which one element of my world — violence — was isolated and made less harmful to me. I am thankful that
I had parents who, instead of imposing literary judgments on my reading, left me alone to do what I needed
to do.

When I talk about the book, then, I am not talking only
about what is ostentatiously called "good" literature. I am
not assigning values to books, decreeing some acceptable
and others not. I am talking about the book as a solitary
voice singing through the vastness, heard by a solitary ear.
It is this that makes the book important. A book has the
capacity to link our solitary souls like pearls on a string
and bring us together into a shared and luminous humanity.

Many years ago, when I lived in New York, I fre-
quented the library near the corner of Twenty-third Street
and Seventh Avenue. I was intrigued by the old women

who came there, especially because all they seemed to read were mysteries and detective novels. I imagined these sweet-looking old women returning to the tiny rooms in which they lived with their cats and ancient teapots, sitting down, and reading gory mysteries, cackling like the witches in *Macbeth,* their teeth dripping blood. It wasn't until I returned to reading mysteries some years later that I understood. Many mystery novels have older women as detectives — Agatha Christie's Miss Marple being the most well known. There is no other literary genre in which older women are treated with dignity, respect, and love. The old women, alone in life, forgotten and useless to society, had found their mirrors and thus mitigated what could have been a crushing loneliness into a solitary warmth.

This is the paradox: Nothing is more solitary an act than reading a book, and yet nothing else invites us into the depths of the solitary where we are no longer alone. It is an act of wizardry, a magic available to us all.

One of the pivotal experiences of my life came when I was eighteen. I wandered into a bookstore in downtown Nashville one frosted, gray day in late autumn aware that I was looking for something: I was looking for myself, and I generally find myself while wandering through a bookstore, looking at books until I find the one that is calling me. On this particular day I wandered for quite a while until I picked up a paperback with the word *Haiku* on the cover. What is that? I wondered. I opened the book and read,

> On a withered branch
> a crow has settled —
> autumn nightfall.

I trembled and turned the pages hastily until my eyes stopped on these words:

    A giant firefly;
        that way, this way, that way, this —
        and it passes by.

I read more of the brief poems, these voices from seventeenth-century Japan, and I knew: This is my voice. This simplicity, this directness, this way of using words to direct the soul to silence and beyond. This is my voice! I exulted inside. Then I stopped. How could I, a little colored kid from Nashville, Tennessee — and that is all I knew myself to be in those days like perpetual death knells — how could I be feeling that something written in seventeenth-century Japan could be my voice?

I almost put the book back, but that inner prompting which had led me to it would not allow such an act of self-betrayal. I bought the book and began writing haiku, and the study of haiku led to the study of Zen Buddhism, which led to the study of flower arranging, and I suspect I am still following the path that opened to me on that day when I was eighteen, though I no longer write haiku.

I eventually understood that it made perfect sense for a little colored kid from Nashville, Tennessee, to recognize his voice in seventeenth-century Japanese poetry. Who we are by the sociological and political definitions of society has little to do with who we are.

In the quiet and stillness that surrounds us when we read a book, we are known to ourselves in ways we are not when we are with people. We enter a relationship of intimacy with the writer, and if the writer has written truly and if we give ourselves over to what is written, we are given the gift of ourselves in ways that surprise and catch the soul off guard.

A book is a beech staff inscribed with runes, plunged into moist earth in a forest clearing. As a writer, I am entrusted with the sacred task of inscribing the staff with runes. It is an enormous responsibility, not to mention an act of daring and risk and presumption.

I wish I could talk to that person in that unknown century who inscribed the beech staff with runes and planted it somewhere for others to read. What did it say? "Don't forget to pick up a package of frozen french fries?" No. If that beech staff gave us our word *book,* then what was inscribed on it was more than a simple message. That person attempted to make his or her carved runes containers for the very universe.

What impelled such an act of presumption? It wasn't ego, certainly. I know that much. Whenever a student says to me, "I think I want to be a writer," my first question is, "Yes, but do you want to write?" Being a writer is a social identity. Carving runes on a beech staff is hard, tedious work. That person carving runes was not impelled by a desire for ego gratification. The urge to create books comes from that same place within us which leads us to read books — the desire for union with another.

Writing is the most solitary kind of work, but it is not an act of self-expression: it is a reaching out to people I do not know and will never know. I sit and type and I see faces — never faces of those I know — and I see rooms, couches, chairs; and I see these unknown people sitting and reading the words flowing through me and onto the screen of my computer. And no matter what I write, I do so because this is the way I am most intimately in relationship with others. The readers of my books receive the best of me. I hope they bring the best of themselves to my words. This solitary act of writing is a social act in which rune carver and reader come together for a while and then part, the better for having known each other — hopefully.

The power of the book does not reside in the information contained in its pages. Computers can hold and transmit more information than a book ever will. But information is not the same as knowledge, because knowledge is more than, other than, facts on a given subject. In the deepest sense, knowledge is even more than erudition and learning, and books are more than the means to be erudite. The word *knowledge* comes to us from a Middle English word that means "to confess, to recognize." Isn't that what the book, almost any book, offers us the opportunity to do — to confess to and recognize ourselves? To confess and recognize our fantasies, our joys and griefs, our aspirations and failures. Deep within the solitary wonder where we sit alone with a book, we confess and recognize what we would be too ashamed to tell another (and sometimes we are as ashamed of joy and delight and success as we are of embarrassment and failure). As a writer and a reader, I come to books for this experience of confession and recognition, and although every book does not afford me this experience, it is the experience all of us seek in the book.

We wander along the densely bordered trails of our lives, trails closed in by meals to be cooked, children whose hurts and joys need our tending (though we may feel scarcely able to tend our own hurts, and joy is something dimly recalled from our youth), marriages that periodically seem to start unraveling before our very eyes and sometimes cannot be knit anew; and there is always the car that needs fixing and the note from American Express telling us to please leave home without it. And lo, in the midst of the minutiae and flotsam of our lives, the trail leads into a small clearing, and there in the center a beech staff stands, plunged into the earth like a sliver of moonbeam, and we stop and read the runes so painfully and painstakingly inscribed thereon; and if the beech staff has been inscribed lovingly, if we can see specks of the writer's blood in the cracks of a few of the runes, we find our heads nodding slowly in amazed recognition that someone else knows. We are confirmed and recognized and say a quiet but audible "Yes, yes. That is how it is."

And that is all a book is, really — the means through which we are led to say yes to ourselves and that densely bordered trail of our lives. The book gives us back to ourselves in a way that nothing else and no one else can, and we return to the trail, a quotation scribbled on a three-by-five card and stuck in our purse or back pocket, and every now and then we pause, take it out and read it aloud, nod our head in amazement anew, and say yes, yes — and smiling, continue on with the mystery of this journey we call our lives.

Memory as a Sacred Act

$\diamond\diamond\diamond$

It is difficult for those of us who work with students to communicate to others how hazardous it is. Its hazards are not those faced by firemen and others who risk physical danger in their jobs. The hazards we face are those of the spirit, hazards all the more real because they cannot be seen.

During my more than two decades in higher education, there has not been a semester I have not faced with dread. During those semesters, there has not been one in which I have not had moments of utter terror, moments of feeling that I have failed.

I walk into the first class of each semester afraid, but not because of any feelings of inadequacy as a teacher. If teaching were merely a job of communicating the given subject matter, I could as easily assign books that first day, come back fourteen weeks later, and give an exam. I wonder sometimes if communicating the subject matter isn't the least of what I do as a teacher, because whether they admit it or not, whether they know it or not, students come into a class seeking the meaning of life. They don't expect to get the answer from me, but they hope that during the semester, something will be said, read, or suspended in the silences that will take them a little closer to the answer.

What is so terrifying about teaching is that each person sitting in the classroom is a human life who has brought with him or her a lifetime of memories that I do not know. And these memories will determine not only how they will learn, but what they will learn, and if they will learn at all. My task is to speak into those memories, though I will never know them.

Perhaps I approach teaching with this attitude because I am a writer, and as a writer, memory is my subject matter. I believe in the named and nameless dead. I believe in the past, not as something completed and forever pinioned to memory but as the accretion of known and unknown lives from whom I came and to whom I am indebted and for whom I am responsible.

For me literature is the faithful psychic record of who and what was. It is a record not of great events, but of the ordinary ones in ordinary lives. Literature is the means through which I share my knowledge of past as present, of past as presence, of past as evermore. This is not a way of looking at literature that I learned, but an experience of life that has been with me since I can remember.

The first fourteen years of my life were lived in Kansas City, Kansas, a small city overshadowed by its larger, sister city, Kansas City, Missouri. The two cities are on opposite banks of the confluence of the Kansas and Missouri rivers, and one of my earliest memories is of driving across the viaduct between the two cities, over that place where the Kansas River flows into the Missouri. In place of the meat-packing plant and airport that actually bordered the rivers, I saw trees and Indians in canoes.

Next to the public library in Kansas City, Kansas, is the burial ground of the Kaw Indians. I remember walking along the broad walkway to the library and looking to my right, to the trees behind which was the Indian burial ground, and I was haunted by a single thought: Who were they? My body was pervaded by an intense sadness that verged on tears because I would never know. However, the sadness was accompanied by a determination to know, because if I could, they would not be as dead, their joys and sorrows would not be so much dust as their bodies were now.

Another memory: It is 1964. I am in Mississippi working with the civil-rights movement. It is a hot day in mid-July and, in a small town called Laurel, I stand at the edge of a vast field. A feeling comes over me and forms itself into a question: What was it like to be a slave and stand where I am standing now? What did that slave feel who stood here one hundred fifty years ago?

Four years later, the questions of that moment crystallized into a book called *To Be a Slave*. Other books, *Long Journey Home* and *This Strange New Feeling,* followed later, each giving answers to that question: What was it like to be a slave?

I spent a lot of hours wondering, what was it like? As a child I tried to imagine: What was it like for de Soto when he first saw the Mississippi River; what was it like when Lewis and Clark saw the Pacific Ocean for the first time; what did those natives on a small island in the Caribbean see when the masts of the *Nina,* the *Pinta,* and the *Santa Maria* came into view over the curved back of the ocean? And what was it like for those unknown and now nameless African ancestors of mine when they were pushed down the plank off a ship and they stood for the first time on the soil of this land?

Sometimes I am ashamed that the dead are more alive for me than many of the living. Perhaps that is because the dead have no one to care for them, to live their lives, their struggles, their triumphs: they have no one to remember. I have often walked through cemeteries, reading the names on the tombstones; the act of reading the names is a ritual of remembrance, and always I ask them: What was it like to be you?

That question is the one that the finest literature seeks to answer. That question is the one the finest literature also poses to us as readers. What is it like to be me?

To write about the past is, then, my way of writing about the present, because nothing I feel has not been felt by many people in many times and places. Loves and hatreds do not change their natures, their ways of entwining in and around people's lives. People who lived in caves knew joy and sorrow. The sight of a herd of buffalo gave them more joy than it would me, but the warmth and elation of joy belongs to all of us.

The most difficult book I've written yet was not an attempt to imagine myself into the lives of cave people but to imagine myself into the life of my own father. The Reverend Joshua Smith, the fictional hero of *Do Lord Remember Me,* had his inception in an odd way. It was August 1981, the day of my father's funeral. We returned to the house from the cemetery and my mother said she wanted me to pack all the things in my father's study. I went in, sat behind his desk, and opened the middle drawer. There I found a manila folder, and in the folder were four or five drafts of his obituary in his handwriting. Suddenly an image came to me of an old black man sitting at his desk trying to set down the facts of his life while knowing that the facts would not add up to his life, and yet, when he was dead, the facts were all that would remain. With that image, it was almost as if my father took possession of me.

Do Lord Remember Me is more fiction than fact, however. It represents not so much my father's biography as his essence, and because of who my father was, his essence represents also the essence of black people's lives in the South, from slavery to the civil-rights movement.

Here lies the paradox at the heart of writing about the dead. Though I write about the dead, I am writing, actually, about you. I know this is true, because you could not read and comprehend what I write if you did not see and experience yourself in what has been written.

Beneath it all, each of us lives, uneasily, with the knowledge that we are doomed to join the named and nameless dead, and it would be no small comfort if we could know that we would be remembered in some small way.

Every year or so I will pick up my grade book and open it to the first page, headed, "Fall, 1971," and I will read the name of every student. I recall many faces with a smile, some with a grimace, and many not at all. But each student is a part of my memory now. The stories many of them shared with me are a part of my story and by caring for their stories, I care for my own.

How many of us have had the experience of being in a city other than our own, or sitting in our office, and someone comes up and says, "Do you remember me?" We have worked out our little formulas for those times we don't have the foggiest notion of who the person is: "I remember your face but you'd better tell me your name." Sometimes, even being told the name does not help. It does not matter. What is important is to honor that need we all have to be remembered, to know that our lives are recalled in the life of someone who mattered to us, that the sacredness of who we are is now a part of the sacredness of someone else.

In the deepest sense, our memories are our lives, and we are very careful with whom we choose to share certain memories, because what we are sharing is who we once were. As a teacher I am surrounded by memory, which is the sacred receptacle of our souls. Our souls touch each other when we give and receive memory.

Literature is a small way of remembering, of honoring

not only the dead but we, the living, who will one day be dead. And once we are dead, it does not matter that we were black or white, male or female. How sad it is that race and gender matter so much while we live.

If literature remembers well and honors well, then perhaps it can teach us, if we are willing to learn, that death makes us equals in every regard. If we allow death to teach us this simple fact, then perhaps, slowly, the quality of our living will begin to change and we will see, as death sees with its hollow sockets, that nothing matters except that we are all human and we die all too soon, never to return, and that we hope, fervently hope, that someone will remember that we were here and we tried our best.

Huckleberry Finn

✧✧✧

I am grateful that among the indignities inflicted on me in childhood I escaped *The Adventures of Huckleberry Finn*. I do not understand how I did, but as carefully as I search the ocean floor of memory, I find no barnacle-encrusted remnant of Huckleberry Finn. But Huck and Tom Sawyer are embedded in the American collective memory like George Washington (about whom I have never read either). Tom and Huck are part of our American selves, a mythologem we imbibe with our mother's milk.

I do remember going to Hannibal, Missouri, with my parents and visiting the two-story, white frame house where Mark Twain lived as a boy, where Huck and Tom lived as boys. In the American collective memory, Twain, Huck, and Tom merge into a paradigm of boyhood that shines as poignantly as a beacon beckoning to us from some paradise lost — albeit no paradise we (or they) ever had.

I remember that house and the white picket fence around it. Maybe it was my father who told me the story about Tom Sawyer painting the fence (if it was Tom who did), and maybe he told me about Huck, too. But it occurs to me only now to wonder if my father ever read Twain's books, my father born in Mississippi when slavery still

83

cast a cold shadow at brightest and hottest noon. And if he did not read Twain, is there any Lester who did? Probably not. But that doesn't matter. Having read the novel finally, I see that in the character of Huckleberry Finn, Twain evoked something sentimentally real in American psyche — something dangerously, fatally seductive.

The summer of 1973, I drove cross-country from New York City, where I was living then, and returned to Hannibal to visit that two-story, white house for the first time since childhood. It was midafternoon when I drove into Hannibal, planning to stay in a motel that night and spend the next morning leisurely going through the Twain boyhood home. As I walked toward the motel desk, there was a noticeable hush among the people in the lobby and I perceived a tightening of many razor-thin, white lips. I was not surprised when the motel clerk said there were no vacancies. The same scenario was repeated at a second and third motel.

It was the kind of situation blacks know a lot about and whites say is merely our imaginations, hypersensitivity, our perceiving discrimination where none exists. (All I know is that between Manhattan and Harding, Montana, Hannibal was the only place I could not find a motel room that summer.) As I drove out of town, another childhood memory returned. It was my father's voice reminding me that "Hannibal is rough on Negroes."

I'd forgotten that, because I had allowed the American collective memory to subsume an inescapable part of black reality. I had permitted myself to be blinded by the image of Huck shining brightly and had been unable to see what was lurking in the shadows.

As a black parent, I am not sympathetic to those black parents who want *The Adventures of Huckleberry Finn* banned from schools. At the same time, I know that my children's education will be enhanced if they are able to avoid the book.

That may sound harsh, but I cannot separate literature, no matter how well written, from morality. By morality I do not mean bourgeois mores that seek to govern the behavior of others in order to create (or coerce) that conformity thought necessary for social cohesion. The truly moral is far broader, far more difficult, and less certain of itself than bourgeois morality, because it is not concerned with the what of behavior but the spirit we bring to our living and, by implication, to literature.

John Gardner put it this way in his book *On Moral Fiction:*

> We recognize true art by its careful, thoroughly honest research for and analysis of values. It is not didactic because, instead of teaching by authority and force, it explores, open-mindedly, to learn what it should teach. It clarifies and confirms. . . . moral art tests values and rouses trustworthy feelings about the better and the worse in human action.

It is in this sense that morality can and should be one of the criteria for assessing literature. It must be if a book is to "serve as the axe for the frozen sea within us," as Kafka wrote. *The Adventures of Huckleberry Finn* is not the axe; it is the frozen sea, immoral in its major premises, one of which demeans blacks and insults history.

Twain makes a parallel between Huck's being "enslaved" by a drunken father who keeps him locked in a cabin and Jim's legal enslavement. Regardless of how awful and wrong it is for a boy to be held physically captive by his father, there is a profound difference between this and slavery. By making them parallelisms, Twain applies a veneer to slavery that obscures the horror it was. Such parallelism also allowed Twain's contemporaries comfortably to evade responsibility and remorse for the horror they had made.

A boy held *captive* by a drunken father is not in the same category as a man *enslaved*. Twain does not appear to understand what it meant to be legally owned by another human being and to have that legal ownership supported by the full power of local, state, and federal governments.

If the novel had been written before Emancipation, Huck's dilemma and conflicting feelings about Jim's escape would have been moving. But, in 1884, slavery was legally over. Huck's almost Hamlet-like interior monologues on the rights and wrongs of helping Jim escape are not proof of liberalism or compassion but evidence of an inability to relinquish whiteness as a badge of superiority. "I knowed he was white inside" is Huck's final assessment of Jim.

Jim does not exist with an integrity of his own. He is a childlike person who, in attitude and character, is more like one of the boys in Tom Sawyer's gang than a grown man with a wife and children — an important fact we do not learn until much later.

The novel plays with black reality from the moment Jim runs away and does not immediately seek his freedom. It defies logic that Jim did not know that Illinois was a free state. Yet, Twain wants us not only to believe that he didn't, but to accept as credible that a runaway slave would sail *south* down the Mississippi River, the only route to freedom he knew being at Cairo, Illinois, where the Ohio River meets the Mississippi. If Jim knew that the Ohio met the Mississippi at Cairo, how could he not have known of the closer proximity of freedom in Illinois to the east or in Iowa to the north?

If the reader must suspend intelligence to accept this,

then intelligence must be dispensed with altogether to believe that Jim, having unknowingly passed the confluence
of the Ohio and Mississippi rivers, would continue down
the river and travel deeper and deeper into the heart of
slave country. Yet, a century of white readers have accepted this.

The least we expect of a novel is that it be credible — if
not wholly in fact then in emotion, for it is emotions that
are the true subject matter of fiction. As Jim floats down
the river farther and farther into slave country, he ex-
presses no anxiety about his fate. He makes no effort to
reverse the situation. Because he doesn't, we enter the
realm of white fantasy where blacks have the humanity of
cabbages.

The novel's climax comes when Jim is sold and Tom
and Huck concoct a ridiculous scheme to free him. During
the course of the rescue, Tom Sawyer is shot. Huck sends
the doctor, who needs assistance to administer to Tom.
Jim comes out of hiding and aids the doctor, knowing he
will be recaptured. The doctor recounts the story this way:

> . . . so I says, I got to have *help* somehow; and the
> minute I says it out crawls this nigger from some-
> wheres and says he'll help, and he done it, too, and
> done it very well. Of course I judged he must be a
> runaway nigger, and there I *was!* and there I had to
> stick right straight along all the rest of the day and
> all night. . . . *I never see a nigger that was a better
> nuss or faithfuler* [emphasis added] and yet he was
> resking his freedom to do it, and was all tired out,
> too, and I see plain enough he'd been worked main
> hard lately. I liked the nigger for that; I tell you,
> gentlemen, a nigger like that is worth a thousand
> dollars — and kind treatment, too . . . there I was

... and there I had to stick till about dawn this morning; then some men in a skiff come by, and as good luck would have it the nigger was setting by the pallet with his head propped on his knees sound asleep; so I motioned them in quiet, and they slipped up on him and grabbed him and tied him before he knowed what he was about, and we never had no trouble ... the nigger never made the least row nor said a word from the start. He ain't no bad nigger, gentlemen; that's what I think about him. (Chap. 42)

This depiction of a black "hero" is familiar by now since it has been repeated in countless novels and films. It is a picture of the only kind of black many whites have ever truly liked — faithful, tending sick whites, not speaking, not causing trouble, and passive. He is the archetypal "good nigger," who lacks self-respect, dignity, and a sense of self separate from the one whites want him to have. A century of white readers have accepted this characterization.

The extent of Twain's contempt for blacks is not revealed fully until Tom Sawyer clears up a matter that had been confusing Huck. When Huck first proposed freeing Jim, he was surprised when Tom agreed. Huck did not know what Tom knew — namely, that Miss Watson had freed Jim when she died two months before.

Once again, credibility is slain. Early in the novel, Jim's disappearance from the town coincides with Huck's. Having manufactured "evidence" of his "murder" to cover his escape from his father, Huck learns that the townspeople believe he was murdered by Jim. Now, we are to believe that an old white woman would free a black suspected of murdering a white child. White people might want and need to believe such fairy tales about themselves, but blacks know better.

But this is not the nadir of Twain's contempt. When Aunt Sally asks Tom why he wanted to free Jim, knowing he was already free, Tom replies: "Well that *is* a question, I must say; and *just* like women! Why, I just wanted the *adventure* of it. . . ." (ibid.). Now Huck understands why Tom was so eager to help Jim "escape."

Tom explains that his plan was "for us to run him down the river on the raft, and have adventures plumb to the mouth of the river." Then he and Huck would tell Jim he was free and take him "back up home on a steamboat, in style, and pay him for his lost time." They would tell everyone they were coming and "get out all the niggers around, and have them waltz him into town with a torchlight procession and a brass-band, and then he would be a hero, and so would we" ("Chapter the Last").

There is no honor here; there is no feeling for or sense of what John Gardner calls that which "is necessary to humanness." Jim is a plaything, an excuse for "the *adventure* of it," to be used as it suits the fancies of the white folk, whether that fancy be a journey on a raft down the river or a torchlight parade. What Jim clearly is not is a human being, and this is emphasized by the fact that Miss Watson's will frees Jim but makes no mention of his wife and children.

Twain doesn't care about the lives the slaves actually lived. Because he doesn't, he devalues the world.

2 ✧✧✧

> *Every hero's proper function is to provide a*
> *noble image for men to be inspired by and*
> *guided by in their own actions; that is, the*
> *hero's business is to reveal what the gods*
> *require and love. . . . the hero's function . . .*
> *is to set the standard in action. . . . the*
> *business of the poet (or "memory" . . .) is*
> *to celebrate the work of the hero, pass the*
> *image on, keep the heroic model of*
> *behavior fresh, generation on generation.*
> JOHN GARDNER,
> *On Moral Fiction*

If it is the hero's task "to reveal what the gods require and love," what do we learn from *The Adventures of Huckleberry Finn?*

The novel's major premise is established in the first chapter:

> The Widow Douglas she took me for her son, and allowed she would sivilize me; but it was rough living in the house all the time, considering how dismal regular and decent the widow was in all her ways; so when I couldn't stand it no longer I lit out. I got into my old rags and my sugar-hogshead again, and was free and satisfied.

Civilization is equated with education, regularity, decency, and being "cramped up" (chap. 6), and the representatives of civilization are women. Freedom is old clothes and doing what you want to do. "All I wanted was a change, I warn't particular" (chap. 1).

That the novel is regarded as a classic tells us much about the psyche of the white American male, because the novel is a powerful evocation of the *puer,* the eternal boy

for whom growth, maturity, and responsibility are enemies. There is no more powerful evocation in American
literature of the eternal adolescent than *The Adventures of
Huckleberry Finn*.

It is a fantasy adolescence, however. Not only is it free
of the usual adolescent problems caused by awakening
sexuality, but Huck has a verbal adroitness and cleverness
beyond the capability of an actual fourteen-year-old. In
Huck, verbal cleverness, lying, and miseducation are exalted. The novel presents admiringly a model of who we
(men) would and could be if not for the pernicious influence of civilization and women.

In his lyrical descriptions of the river and life on the
raft, Twain creates an almost primordial yearning for a life
of freedom from responsibility.

> It was kind of solemn, drifting down the big, still
> river, laying on our backs looking up at the stars,
> and we didn't even feel like talking loud, and it
> warn't often that we laughed — only a little kind of
> low chuckle. We had mighty good weather as a gen-
> eral thing, and nothing ever happened to us at
> all. . . . (Chap. 12)

> Sometimes we'd have that whole river all to our-
> selves for the longest time. Yonder was the banks
> and the islands, across the water; and maybe a
> spark — which was a candle in a cabin window; and
> sometimes on the water you could see a spark or
> two — on a raft or a scow, you know; and maybe
> you could hear a fiddle or a song coming over from
> one of them crafts. It's love to live on a raft. We had
> the sky up there, all speckled with stars, and we used
> to lay on our backs and look up at them, and discuss
> about whether they was made or only just hap-
> pened. . . . (Chap. 19)

It is in passages such as these that the book is most seductive in its quiet singing of the "natural" life over the one of "sivilization," which is another form of slavery for Huck. It is here also that the novel fails most as moral literature.

Twain's notion of freedom is the simplistic one of freedom from restraint and responsibility. It is an adolescent vision nowhere more clearly expressed than in the often-quoted and much admired closing sentences of the novel:

> But I reckon I got to light out for the territory ahead of the rest, because Aunt Sally she's going to adopt me and sivilize me, and I can't stand it. I been there before.

That's just the problem, Huck. You haven't "been there before." Then again, neither have too many other white American males, and that's the problem, too. They persist in clinging to the teat of adolescence long after only blood oozes from the nipples. They persist in believing that freedom from restraint and responsibility represents paradise. The paradox is that this is a mockery of freedom, a void. We express the deepest caring for this world and ourselves only by taking responsibility for ourselves and whatever portion of this world we make ours.

Twain's failure is that he does not care until it hurts. Because he doesn't, his contempt for humanity is disguised as satire, as humor. No matter how charming and appealing Huck is, Twain holds him in contempt. Here we come to the other paradox, the crucial one that white Americans have so assiduously resisted: It is not possible to regard blacks with contempt without having first so regarded yourselves.

To be moral. It takes an enormous effort of will to be moral, and that's another paradox. Only to the extent that we make the effort to be moral do we grow away from adolescent notions of freedom and begin to see that the true nature and contour of freedom does not lie in "lighting out for the territory ahead" but resides where it always has — in the territory within.

Only there does one begin to live with one's self with that seriousness from which genuine humor and satire are born. Twain could not explore the shadowy realms of slavery and freedom with integrity because he did not risk becoming a person. Only by doing so could he have achieved real compassion. Then, Jim could have been a man and Huck would have been a boy and we, the readers, would have learned a little more about the territory ahead that is always within.

James Baldwin
(1924–1987)
✧✧✧

With the publication of *The Price of the Ticket: Collected Nonfiction 1948–1985*, James Baldwin presented the work on which he wanted to be judged and remembered. That came to fifty-one essays, twenty-five of them previously uncollected. The remaining twenty-six represented the contents of five previously published books: *Notes of a Native Son, Nobody Knows My Name, The Fire Next Time, No Name in the Street*, and *The Devil Finds Work*.

Arranged chronologically from February 1948 to January 1985, the essays are often overpowering in their intensity and brilliance. In the essays of the first fifteen years, Baldwin wrote not only as a black writer pleading the cause of blacks but as a black pleading the cause of humanity — and what an eloquent humanist he was.

> But our humanity is our burden, our life; we need not battle for it; we need only to do what is infinitely more difficult — that is, accept it. The failure of the protest novel lies in its rejection of life, the human being, the denial of his beauty, dread, power, in its

insistence that it is his categorization alone which is real and which cannot be transcended. ("Everybody's Protest Novel," 1949)

Sometimes, Baldwin startled and confused by using "we" as if he were white.

Our dehumanization of the Negro then is indivisible from our dehumanization of ourselves: the loss of our own identity is the price we pay for our annulment of his. ("Many Thousands Gone," 1951)

From 1948 to 1963, Baldwin's message was more moral than political, more psychological than ideological, and it had two central elements: (1) the necessity for blacks to free themselves from white-imposed definitions, and (2) the necessity for whites to free themselves from their own definitions. As long as this mutual interdependence was unrecognized, blacks and whites could not be human to themselves. If one cannot be human to oneself, it is impossible to be human to another.

It is a terrible, an inexorable, law that one cannot deny the humanity of another without diminishing one's own: in the face of one's victim, one sees oneself. ("Fifth Avenue Uptown," 1960)

The early Baldwin did not hesitate to condemn the West for its sins, but he did not offer simplistic political solutions as the means of redemption.

That image one is compelled to hold of another person — in order . . . to retain one's image of oneself — may become that person's trial, his cross, his death. It may or may not become his prison: but it inevitably becomes one's own. People who thought of Bessie Smith as a coarse black woman, and who

let her die, were far less free than Bessie, who had
escaped all their definitions by becoming herself.
This is still the only way to become a man or a
woman — or an artist. ("On Catfish Row," 1956)

Baldwin's most enduring book, *The Fire Next Time,*
was published in 1963, the year Bull Connor unleashed
police dogs and fire hoses on blacks demonstrating in
Birmingham, Alabama. The images were shown on the
nightly news; northern whites were horrified and the treatment of blacks in the South became a concern of the national conscience.

In *The Fire Next Time,* Baldwin combined anger and
humanism in a way that whites could receive the anger not
as an unqualified condemnation of themselves but as angry tears of righteousness seeking to save us all.

. . . if the word *integration* means anything, this is
what it means; that we, with love, shall force our
brothers to see themselves as they are, to cease
fleeing from reality and begin to change it. . . . We
cannot be free until they are free.

Here is the James Baldwin whose voice was the literary
equivalent of Martin Luther King, Jr. — the James Baldwin
who sought to make whites and blacks take responsibility
for not only their own humanity but that of the other.

While *The Fire Next Time* was the most eloquent
expression of Baldwin's humanism, within its pages there
was a small but perceptible shift in attitude.

I could not share the white man's vision of himself
for the very good reason that white men in America
do not behave toward black men the way they behave toward each other.

But is that true? "One cannot deny the humanity of another without diminishing one's own," Baldwin had written a few years earlier. If that is so (and I believe that it is), then white men in America do "behave toward each other" in the same way they behave toward blacks. They must, because how we treat others is only a reflection of how we treat ourselves.

What was hinted at in *The Fire Next Time* and would become more evident in the years after was Baldwin's inability to bear any longer the unresolvable tension of that ambiguous "we." Perhaps the wonder is that he bore it as long as he did. It is not easy for a black person to identify with the Stars and Stripes, to see his or her fate as inseparable from that of white Americans. But neither do whites have the fortitude to withstand the complexity of that inclusive American "we."

At some point in the mid-to-late sixties, Baldwin suffered a failure of moral nerve and took refuge behind the lofty label "witness." When he did, his vision narrowed. He ceased struggling with the "we" and became a prisoner of race.

2 ✧✧✧

Witness.

That is how Baldwin described himself. Not many writers would be comfortable with that self-definition, or understand it.

"I am a witness to whence I came, where I am, witness to what I've seen and the possibilities that I think I see," Baldwin said when I interviewed him for the *New York Times Book Review* of May 27, 1984.

I began using the word when I began to be called a spokesman. I'm certainly not a spokesman, and the only word I could find is that I'm trying to be a witness. A spokesman assumes that he is speaking for others. I never assumed that I could. What I tried to do, or to interpret and make clear, was that what the republic was doing to black people, it was doing to itself. No society can smash the social contract and be exempt from the consequences, and the consequences are chaos for everybody in the society. In the church in which I was raised, you were supposed to bear witness to the truth. Now, of course, later on, you wonder what in the world the truth is, but you do know what a lie is.

To be a witness is a dangerous undertaking because it imposes upon us the responsibility to know that we are seeing all that is there. Additionally, it imposes on us the responsibility to know that what we are seeing is true.

While Baldwin was willing to "wonder what in the world the truth is," how could he be so certain that "you do know what a lie is." It is this absolute certainty that gives Baldwin's writing its urgency, passion, and moral power, a power so compelling that it is almost seductive.

But this is both the appeal and the danger the moralist presents. For the moralist, truth and falsehood are irreconcilable opposites. Such certainty gives those who listen the womblike security that comes when one belongs to a cause.

Truth, however, is not without ambiguity. It has wrinkles and shadows, and while it may look attractive by the light of morning, at dusk one hesitates to reach down and pick it up because there can be no certainty about what may be hidden beneath. Truth has many textures and colors, and when they are placed next to one another the whole is not necessarily as appealing as a quilt sewn by a grandmother in Mississippi.

That tone of unassailable moral righteousness so characteristic of Baldwin's nonfiction makes you feel that you are on the side of the angels. There lies the danger. If you are on the side of the angels, there must be devils on the other side. The challenge of the ambiguous "we" and the task in being human is learning how to stand between the angels and the devils and taking sides with neither.

The major turning point in Baldwin's career was his decision to use his literary and speaking ability in the black political movement of the sixties. Privately, Baldwin talked more than once about a conversation he'd had with Ralph Ellison in which Ellison advised him to remain politically uninvolved. I asked Baldwin about this when I interviewed him for the *New York Times Book Review*.

JL: Ralph Ellison said something to you once about the writer not being involved in politics — that the writer should not be involved in politics.

JB: This is hard work. You never think about these things — if you can help it. Well, in terms of Ralph's advice to me, I agreed with it. I could see what he meant. It's only in retrospect that I can say that my return to America from France to go on what we know now was the civil-rights road — only in retrospect can I say that that was a political act. At the time, it was simply hygienic. It was something I had to do to live with myself. I could not possibly have sat in Paris any longer talking about the Negro problem and looking at photographs of the Negro kids going to school, or trying to go to school. For me it was simpler to go home.

Ralph and I had that conversation, if memory
serves, when I came back from my first trip
South in 1957. I was down there a long time, so
the conversation with Ralph would be in 1958.
I may even have brought the subject up. I think
I did, 'cause it was very much on my mind. The
only reaction I could have had to what he said
is, that's very probably true. But I didn't see how
I could avoid it. But I had to take that chance. I
do not see how I couldn't. I did what I had to
do. I supposed that if I was any good as a writer,
that if my talent meant anything, it would have
to survive it. If not, then, too bad. (Unpublished
transcript)

Ralph Ellison chose to maintain the tension of the
"we." In his second collection of essays, *Going to the Territory,* he asserted the concept of American democracy
over that of blackness and ethnicity. He rejected racial
identity as a sine qua non and insisted on affirming
"American diversity," which he described as a "complex of
intermixing," of races, regions, and religions.

The crucial question is not one of having a perfect
society, or even of having at any given moment a viable — as they say — society. Rather, it is to keep
struggling, to keep trying to reduce to consciousness
all of the complex experience which ceaselessly un-
folds within this great nation. ("On Initiation Rites
and Power," 1969)

America is a unique experiment in social organization — not a nation built on a homogeneity of race, religion, or culture, but an experiment and adventure in creating a whole from the virtues and liabilities of every race,
religion, and culture. And it is the racial politics of Amer-

ica that prevents Americans from looking at each other and seeing what truly is.

By pushing significant details of our experience into the underground of unwritten history, we not only overlook much which is positive, but we blur our conceptions of where and who we are. Not only do we confuse our moral identity, but by ignoring such matters as the sharing of bloodlines and cultural traditions by groups of widely differing ethnic origins, and by overlooking the blending and metamorphosis of cultural forms which is so characteristic of our society, we misconceive our cultural identity. ("Going to the Territory," 1979)

For Ellison, the promise of America is that it relieves us "of the burden of interpreting all of life and its works in racial terms. . . . We've been in such haste to express our anger and our pain as to allow the single tree of race to obscure our view of the magic forest of art."

Such words have not made Ellison a black cultural icon among those mesmerized by what he has called "blood magic and blood thinking." Too, Ellison's cool writing style — its elegance, its absence of angry introspection, its refusal to condemn whites and America for real and imagined sins — ensures that he will be ignored by those who need to hear him most.

But Ellison was not a man of his times in the way Baldwin was; that is, Ellison chose not to become identified with and become the voice for the prevailing black collective. Ellison seems to have willfully kept himself apart from the sixties, because of his belief that the artist owes his allegiance to that in the human being which endures through every time.

Baldwin made another choice, one more complicated than becoming the witness he saw himself as. After *The*

Fire Next Time, his vision of blacks as victims slowly gained precedence over the humanistic one. But this fits with his being a moral witness, because there is no more unassailable paradigm of truth than the victim. No one can speak with more unassailable authority than he who suffers, than he whose wounds bleed for all to see, than he whose suffering is a condemnation of those who do not suffer as he does. The victim appropriates all righteousness to himself because of what was and is being done to him. What the victim wins is personal and collective identity (the two are one for the victim) and moral superiority.

Baldwin never questioned or doubted that what he was witness to represented more than the autobiographical landscape of his emotions. He would see, more and more, only what he wished to see, and would struggle less and less with the complexity of what was.

In *The Fire Next Time,* the humanistic Baldwin wrote of his concern for the "dignity" of blacks and for the "health" of their souls, declaring that he

> must oppose any attempt that Negroes may make to do to others what has been done to them. . . . It is so simple a fact and one that is so hard, apparently, to grasp: *Whoever debases others is debasing himself* [Baldwin's italics]. This is not a mystical statement but a realistic one, which is proved by the eyes of any Alabama sheriff — and I would not like to see Negroes ever arrive at so wretched a condition.

After *The Fire Next Time,* Baldwin did not "oppose any attempt" of blacks "to do to others" what had "been done to them." He did not oppose the rhetorical excesses of the black-power movement in the late sixties, nor did he seek to examine the meaning of Louis Farrakhan, the glint of whose eyes bears no small resemblance to those "of any Alabama sheriff."

Baldwin was quite eloquent when articulating that the salvation for whites was to take responsibility for the evil they had wrought.

> It has always been much easier (because it has always seemed much safer) to give a name to the evil without than to locate the terror within. And yet, the terror within is far truer and far more powerful than any of our labels: the labels change, the terror is constant. ("Nothing Personal," 1964)

Baldwin did not, however, take the next step and say that blacks, too, must take responsibility, not only for the evil they have wrought, but even for the evil they have endured. Blacks must take responsibility for the terrors with which they live — terrors that, more often than not these days, they project onto whites as surely as whites project their terrors onto blacks.

But Baldwin was unable to ask blacks to take responsibility for their evil and their terror. He had become a witness; that is, he had chosen to be the persecuted one, the victim.

When I interviewed him, I asked if Richard Wright had had a responsibility to him and if he had a responsibility to younger black writers.

JB: I never felt that Richard had a responsibility for me, and if he had, he'd discharged it. What I was thinking about, though, was the early fifties, when the world was breaking up, when the world of white supremacy was breaking up. I'm talking about the revolutions all over the world, specifically since we were in Paris — Tunisia, Algeria, the ferment in Senegal, the French loss of their Indochinese empire. A whole lot of

people — darker people for the most part —
came from all kinds of places to Richard's door,
as they do now to my door. And in that sense he
had a responsibility which he didn't know — well,
who can blame him? A boy from Ethiopia, a
boy from Senegal, a boy from — they all claimed
him. They had the right to claim him, like they
have the right to claim me.

JL: What's that right? Why did they have the right
to claim him? Why do they have the right to
claim you?

JB: Well, right or not, there he was to be claimed.
He was the most articulate black witness of his
moment. And you can hardly blame a boy from
Ethiopia, or a boy from Senegal, or a boy from
Algeria for expecting Richard to understand
what their situation was in Paris. Richard and I
had a quarrel — well, it wasn't a quarrel — but
I said to Richard many times that Paris might
have been the city of refuge for him. It might
have been a city of refuge for me, but it wasn't
that for anybody from Senegal, Algeria, or
Tunisia. Richard was known in Paris and they
had a right to claim him, much more right than
those who did claim him — Sartre, de Beauvoir,
et cetera.

But that, ultimately, was between Richard
and Richard. I was in a very funny position. The
people who knocked on his door ended up sleep-
ing on my floor. I knew something about it
which Richard didn't know. Does that make
sense to you?

JL: I'm not certain. This may be one of those generational things. What is this claim that you say black people have on you?

JB: I see what you're saying. But it's not only black people, if you like. You're suggesting that there's something unjust in it. There is something unjust in it —

JL: Yes, there is.

JB: — but it's an irreducible injustice, I think. I found no way around it. But you can't execute the responsibility in the way the people who want you to execute it want you to do it. You can't answer in the language that they think they want you to answer. You have to do your work. But, at the same time, you're out there. You asked for it. And no matter how you react to it, you cannot pretend that it is not happening. I know in my own case that there is no place in the world that I can go — including Helsinki, which is where I learned it the first time — where the darker brother will not claim you, because you represent him. At least according to him. I don't think I represent him according to me. (Unpublished transcript)

His denials and especially his final sentence were not convincing. I pressed him, asking if he ever resented being expected "to represent the darker brother."

JB: Oh, it has given me some trying moments, but not for long. I say to myself, "It comes with the territory." It is not my fault and it is not their fault that the world thinks it's white. Therefore

someone who is not white and has managed to
survive somehow and attempts to be in some
way responsible — of course you're going to be
claimed by multitudes of black kids. There's no
way around it. How you react to it is one thing.
Just or unjust is irrelevant. That's the way it is.
I've never been to Algeria, for example, but I'm
told I'm a hero there. I can believe it.

But could you be claimed without being enslaved eventually by those who claimed you? Could you be claimed
without eventually relinquishing something of your soul?

In *No Name in the Street* (1972), Baldwin's voice is a
black collective one. There is not an individual speaking,
only a historical force.

In the early pages of the book, Baldwin tells a story
about a suit he bought to wear at a Carnegie Hall appear-
ance with Martin Luther King, Jr., and how, two weeks
later, he wore it at King's funeral. Baldwin mentioned to
columnist Leonard Lyons that he could never wear the suit
again. Lyons printed Baldwin's comment in his column.

A few days later, Baldwin received a call from a childhood friend asking if he could have the suit Jimmy had
worn only twice and wouldn't wear again. Baldwin gave
his friend the suit because

that bloody suit was *their* suit. . . . it had been
bought *for* them, it had even been bought *by* them:
they had created Martin, he had not created them,
and the blood in which the fabric of that suit was
stiffening was theirs.

Literally, of course, there was no blood on the suit, but
the hyperbole permits Baldwin to exalt blacks (and him-

self) as victims. There are no individuals any longer, only the martyred race.

No Name in the Street is stunning for its lack of insight into the dangers represented by the Black Panther party. Baldwin saw the Panthers as a "great force for peace and stability in the ghetto, . . . a force working toward the health and liberation of the community." Why was Baldwin unable to see that the Panthers were a street gang who had found themselves a good hustle? (And by 1972, this was a view being offered by other writers.)

In the essays of the seventies and eighties, Baldwin becomes the voice of an "us" against a "them," and he ceases to demand that blacks risk the terror and burden of being human, as he still demands of whites.

His review of Alex Haley's *Roots* could have been written by any black writer beating the drum of blackness. At the end of the review, one sees the philosophical consequences of allowing one's self to be claimed: "It [*Roots*] suggests, with great power, how each of us, however unconsciously, can't but be the vehicle of the history which has produced us."

It is the statement of one who sees himself as a victim, someone who would reduce history to determinism. By so doing, the individual does not have to take responsibility for what he or she does with history. Baldwin's statement can be used to justify racism, because whites are as much the vehicles of "the history which has produced us" as are blacks. But that is the logical conclusion of the witness-as-martyr: eventually, everyone is a victim.

Everyone, that is, except Jews.

The most disturbing of the later essays is "An Open Letter to the Born Again" (1979), written in the bitter aftermath of Andrew Young's resignation as United Nations ambassador, at a time when black leaders excoriated

Jews for their perceived role in that resignation. It is not Baldwin's first statement on blacks and Jews, but it is the one that leaves no doubt about an anti-Semitic thread in his writings.

3 ✧✧✧

"The Harlem Ghetto" (1948), Baldwin's first essay on blacks and Jews, presents a picture of an ambivalent relationship. Through the Old Testament, blacks identify with Jews and even consider themselves Jews because of how they have suffered. On the other hand, Jews "include all infidels of white skin who have failed to accept the Savior."

Outside the domain of theology, however, Jews are seen as the "small tradesmen" of Harlem who "operate in accordance with the American business tradition of exploiting Negroes, and they are therefore identified with oppression and are hated for it." Added to this is the black attitude that decrees "that the Jew should 'know better,' that he has suffered enough himself to know what suffering means."

Baldwin is not optimistic about black-Jewish relations because "the structure of the American commonwealth has trapped both these minorities into attitudes of perpetual hostility." And here, Baldwin has made a subtle shift, placing responsibility on something called "the structure of the American commonwealth."

He concludes that "both the Negro and the Jew are helpless; the pressure of living is too immediate and incessant to allow time for understanding."

The essay ends with what will become Baldwin's basic attitude toward blacks and Jews.

The Negro, facing a Jew, hates, at bottom, not his Jewishness but the color of his skin. It is not the Jewish tradition by which he has been betrayed but the tradition of his native land. But just as a society must have a scapegoat, so hatred must have a symbol. Georgia has the Negro and Harlem has the Jew.

Anti-Semitism is present in the essay but is so subtle as to be almost unnoticeable. That is because Baldwin's anti-Semitism is usually not in what he wrote. Indeed, Baldwin would make a point of denouncing anti-Semitism and presenting himself as friendly to Jews. The anti-Semitism lies in a one-sidedness, a failure to measure and judge blacks as he did Jews.

While Baldwin is willing to talk about the assumption "that the Jew should 'know better,'" why is there not the correlative assumption that blacks, too, should know better? Is there not a correlative demand that because blacks know what it is like to be collectively condemned, they are obligated not to collectively condemn others?

Baldwin writes about the Jew-as-merchant "exploiting Negroes" and presents this stereotype as objective truth. Are we to believe that Italian, Irish, or black merchants do not "exploit Negroes," whatever that means.

Baldwin seems unconscious of the irony of his final sentence: "Georgia has the Negro and Harlem has the Jew." One could conclude that the blacks of Harlem and the whites of Georgia have a lot in common — they are both racist.

The most famous Baldwin essay on blacks and Jews is "Negroes Are Anti-Semitic Because They're Anti-White" (1967).

[In my original version of this piece, I quoted extensively from this particular essay of Baldwin's, because I wanted to be fair to him. I also wanted readers to have the opportunity to compare Baldwin's words and my analysis side by side so as to better reach their own conclusions. But since my direct quotes exceeded what might have been considered legally as "fair use," the Baldwin estate refused to grant me permission to quote him as extensively as his views deserve. While I believe that I have paraphrased fairly, nothing is more fair than a person's own words, and I regret being unable to include as much of Baldwin himself as I would have liked.]

From the opening sentence, the tone is harsher and more angry than that of the 1948 essay.

"When we were growing up in Harlem our demoralizing series of landlords were Jewish, and we hated them." Who is the "we"? Is it the Baldwin family? Is it all blacks who lived in Harlem at that time and, by implication, all blacks everywhere?

Very quickly, Baldwin paints a picture of a life surrounded by hostile Jews. Not only was the landlord Jewish, but so was the grocer, "and being in debt to him was very much like being in debt to the company store." This analogy carries associations to coal miners enslaved by indebtedness to the company that owned the mine. Exactly to whom or what the Jewish grocers of Harlem "enslaved" blacks by giving them credit is not said, however. The butcher was also a Jew and not only did "we" pay him more "for bad cuts of meat, . . . we very often carried insults home, along with the meat." The sellers of clothes and shoes were also Jewish, as was, of course, the pawnbroker, who was perhaps "hated most of all."

Baldwin writes that the merchants on 125th Street, Harlem's main business strip, were "Jewish — at least many of them were. . . ." Then comes the first direct expression of anti-Semitism: "I don't know if Grant's or Woolworth's are Jewish names. . . ." Why didn't James

Baldwin bother to do a little research to find out if Grant's and Woolworth's were owned by Jews? But what would it mean if they were?

Baldwin retreats a little and acknowledges that "not all of these white people were cruel. . . ." Some were "as thoughtful as the bleak circumstances allowed. . . ." There is an odd shift here from describing the people as Jews to describing them as white. But kindnesses or not, Baldwin concludes, "all of them were exploiting us, and that was why we hated them."

If the exploitation gave rise to the hatred, then what purpose is served by calling the people Jews? Baldwin tacitly acknowledges this, because as he continues his catalog of exploiters — police and teachers — he acknowledges that not only were not all of them Jews, some were blacks.

But there is a shift back when he recounts going to the union hall to pay his father's union dues and recalls hating the union leaders for taking money from "that envelope which contained bread for his children." Baldwin concludes the paragraph with this sentence: "But whether or not all these people were Jewish, I really do not know." The implied "truth" is the opposite, however.

There is a rhetorical irresponsibility in that sentence, which is only a prelude to a discordant litany, beginning with the statement "The Army may or may not be controlled by Jews: I don't know and I don't care." What Baldwin does know is that when he worked for the Army he hated his bosses because of how they treated him. Baldwin maintains that he doesn't know if the post office is Jewish, but he wouldn't want to work for it again. The list of establishments he worked for, hated, and which he isn't sure are Jewish, continues: Wanamaker's department store, Nabisco, Riker's. The list concludes with people he hated, who he also isn't sure are Jewish: a white man who used to call him "Shine" until Baldwin tried to kill him, and the last taxicab driver who wouldn't pick him up.

Are we supposed to believe that James Baldwin does not know if the Army is controlled by Jews? Are we supposed to believe that James Baldwin does not know if the post office is controlled by Jews? The implication of each of his "I don't knows" is to hint at Jewish control, and by linking that control with his hatred of the particular jobs, he makes Jews responsible for his perceived victimization.

Baldwin's attitude toward his jobs is a precious one, as if no one but him ever had such jobs, as if no one except him ever hated such jobs, as if he is the only one who ever hated his boss.

Baldwin continues and he is "generous" enough to concede that he doesn't "think" that General Electric or any of the other major corporations, Wall Street, or any of the major cities "are controlled by Jews." Baldwin thinks they are controlled "by Americans" and the condition of blacks in America stems from this "control." Black anti-Semitism is really confirmation of this control. "It is not the Jew who controls the American drama," he concludes the first part of the essay. "It is the Christian."

The conclusion to the first part of the essay is fraught with imprecise language and thinking. In what ways is the "American Negro situation . . . a direct result of this control," and what precisely is "this control"? Baldwin does not say.

The next part of the essay purports to show that "anti-Semitism among Negroes is, ironically, the relationship of colored peoples — all over the globe — to the Christian world." However, the condition of blacks "will not be ameliorated — in fact, it can only be aggravated — by the adoption on the part of colored people now, of the most devastating of the Christian vices" — that is, anti-Semitism.

Having established his "credentials," Baldwin criticizes

what he calls the "many Jews" who "use, shamelessly, the slaughter of the six million by the Third Reich as proof that they cannot be bigots — or in the hope of not being held responsible for their bigotry." The key word is "shamelessly." Baldwin has appropriated a divine omniscience. He goes on and tells us that

> it is galling to be told by a Jew whom you know to be exploiting you that he cannot possibly be doing what you know he is doing because he is a Jew. It is bitter to watch the Jewish storekeeper locking up his store for the night, and going home. Going, with your money in his pocket, to a clean neighborhood, miles from you, which you will not be allowed to enter.

Baldwin does not tell us if it was also bitter to watch the black storekeeper and the Italian and Irish storekeepers lock up their stores and leave "with your money in his pocket."

That some of the money might be given to civil-rights organizations only makes matters worse for Baldwin. ". . . this money can be looked on as conscience money, as money given to keep the Negro happy, in his place, and out of white neighborhoods." The assertion is not only cynical to the extreme; it is hateful.

Baldwin says that American Jewish suffering is not "as great as the American Negro's suffering" for a number of reasons. One is because

> the Jew can be proud of his suffering, or at least not ashamed of it. His history and his suffering do not begin in America, where black men have been taught to be ashamed of everything, especially their suffering.

Like an ambulance siren, there it is — the whine of the victim. "Black men have been taught to be ashamed of everything. . . ." (Do not blacks bear some responsibility for having *learned* "to be ashamed of everything"?) However, Baldwin asserts that Jewish suffering is recognized as a part of "the moral history of the world," that Jews are recognized as contributors to world history and the same is not true for blacks. Then he appears to qualify these statements by writing that whether or not one can say that Jewish history is honored, one can say that it is known. Not only is black history unknown, it has been consistently disparaged.

Baldwin writes as if Jews are to blame that their suffering has been recognized "as part of the moral history of the world." Of course, many Jews would dispute that this is so, and in 1967, the Holocaust had not made its way into the history books, nor were publishers eager to publish the stories of survivors. But that is almost beside the point. Baldwin is intent on blaming Jews for their virtues as well as their sins.

> The Jew is a white man, and when white men rise up against oppression, they are heroes; when black men rise, they have reverted to their native savagery. The uprising in the Warsaw ghetto was not described as a riot, nor were the participants maligned as hoodlums. . . . But, of course, my comparison of Watts and Harlem with the Warsaw ghetto will be immediately dismissed as outrageous.

What is sad is that someone as intelligent as Baldwin could be so ignorant about the Warsaw-ghetto uprising. When all the blacks of New York City are forced by armed troops to live in Harlem and Harlem is sealed off and ringed by troops, and when thousands of blacks are taken each day and sent to extermination camps, then Harlem can be compared to the Warsaw ghetto. Equally vulgar is Baldwin's comparison of the Warsaw-ghetto resistance and the rioters of Harlem and Watts. The former were fighting, literally, to save themselves from mass extermination.

But Baldwin does not respect that there are important distinctions in the particulars of black and Jewish suffering. Instead, he denigrates and falsifies the Jewish experience in his effort to be morally superior.

Baldwin contends that few Americans take the black condition seriously, that for every successful black, hundreds more will perish, "because the Republic despises their dreams."

> . . . if one is a Negro in Watts or Harlem, and knows why one is there, and knows that one has been sentenced to remain there for life, one can't but look on the American state and the American people as one's oppressors. For that, after all, is exactly what they are. They have corralled you where you are for their ease and their profit, and are doing all in their power to prevent you from finding out enough about yourself to be able to rejoice in the only life you have.

Once again, blacks are portrayed as helpless victims, as people who have no responsibility, not even for being able to rejoice in their lives. Baldwin is no longer interested in the complex whole of human experience. Truth resides exclusively in the black experience. He tells us that the indigenous peoples of the Belgian Congo endured unspeakable atrocities at the hands of Belgians, "at the hands of Europe," and they endured these atrocities in silence. Their suffering, says Baldwin, was not "indignantly reported in the western press," as the suffering of whites surely would have been.

Baldwin could not so gaily wrap himself in the bloodied victim's rags if he had been honest enough to remember that the Holocaust was "at the hands of Europe" and it was not "indignantly reported in the western press" either.

Baldwin concludes by asserting that black anti-Semitism condemns "the Jew for having become an American white man — for having become, in effect, a Christian." Blacks single out Jews not because they act differently from other whites, but because they don't. The Jew's major distinction is given him by the history of Christendom, which has victimized both blacks and Jews. In Harlem the Jew is playing the role assigned him by Christians long ago, i.e., that of the middleman, the one who does the Christian's dirty work. Baldwin maintains that the Jew is part of the history of Europe, and that is how he will always be considered by the descendants of slaves.

Baldwin's anti-Semitism is not the virulent Jew-hating rhetoric we are accustomed to defining as anti-Semitic expression. And Baldwin's reputation is such that it is almost blasphemous to say that anti-Semitism is an element in his writings on blacks and Jews.

It is there, and Baldwin himself was never able to see it because he thought that his description of Jewish reality was, in fact, Jewish reality. "The Jew must see that he is part of the history of Europe," Baldwin self-righteously announces. He forgets that part of the history of Europe — the greater part — saw Jews being ghettoized and massacred as killers of Christ. How can Baldwin ignore the fact that one-third of the Jews of Europe were killed during the Third Reich?

Baldwin lost the capacity and patience for complexity. When one can no longer tolerate complexity, the moral sense suffers and becomes one-sided and self-righteous. Baldwin's "explanation" of black anti-Semitism is an attempt to justify it, because Baldwin does not warn against the effects of anti-Semitism on blacks as he warns in other essays about the effects of racism on whites.

Baldwin presents a picture of Jews that declares "how I see you is who you are." He who loses the capacity for complexity has lost the capacity to love his ignorance.

This is evident in the 1979 "Open Letter to the Born Again." First, those familiar with "Negroes Are Anti-Semitic Because They're Anti-White" will be stunned by the following passage:

> The first white man I ever saw was the Jewish manager who arrived to collect the rent, and he collected the rent because he did not own the building. I never, in fact, saw any of the people who owned any of the buildings in which we scrubbed and suffered for so long, until I was a grown man and famous. None of them were Jews.

One is not disturbed when a writer appears to contradict himself because his opinions have changed. But statements of fact are not supposed to change. The opening paragraph of "Negroes Are Anti-Semitic Because They're Anti-White" reads:

> When we were growing up in Harlem our demoralizing series of landlords were Jewish, and we hated them. We hated them because they were terrible landlords, and did not take care of the building. A coat of paint, a broken window, a stopped sink, a stopped toilet, a sagging floor, a broken ceiling, a dangerous stairwell, the question of garbage disposal, the question of heat and cold, of roaches and

rats — all questions of life and death for the poor, and especially for those with children — we had to cope with all of these as best we could. Our parents were lashed down to futureless jobs, in order to pay the outrageous rent. We knew that the landlord treated us this way only because we were colored, and he knew that we could not move out.

What is the truth? In the 1967 essay, being in debt to the grocer was "like being in debt to the company store." In the 1979 essay, however,

the grocer and the druggist were Jews . . . and they were very nice to me, and to us. They were never really white, for me. The cops were white. The city was white. The threat was white, and God was white. Not for even a split second in my life did the despicable, utterly cowardly accusation that "the Jews killed Christ" reverberate. I knew a murderer when I saw one, and the people who were trying to kill me were not Jews.

One did not have this impression from reading the 1967 essay.

What is going on becomes clear in the next paragraph.

But the State of Israel was not created for the salvation of the Jews; it was created for the salvation of the Western interest. This is what is becoming clear (I must say that it was always clear to me). The Palestinians have been paying for the British colonial policy of "divide and rule" and for Europe's guilty Christian conscience for more than thirty years.

Now it is obvious why the Jews of Baldwin's Harlem are suddenly good guys. This was Baldwin's way of "establishing" that he did not have a personal animus against Jews and thus giving himself legitimacy for his attack on Israel. His propensity for cosmic generalizations leads him to conclude that

> the Jew, in America, is a white man. He has to be, since I am a black man, and, as he supposes, his only protection against the fate which drove him to America. But he is still doing the Christian's dirty work, and black men know it.

Baldwin simply will not permit Jews to have any reality except that which he, as the voice of black people, will permit them.

Complexity and honesty demand, however, that one be attentive to and take into account how a people view their own history and experience. Indeed, in Baldwin's early essays there are noble statements that argue against defining others solely on the basis of one's own experience, essays that challenge us to live on the razor's edge of risk and vulnerability.

But having permitted himself to be claimed by blacks, he abdicated the lonely responsibility of the artist and intellectual — the responsibility to be claimed by nothing but the futile and beautiful quest for truth.

In 1962 Baldwin wrote:

> The truth, in spite of appearances and all our hopes, is that everything is always changing and the measure of our maturity as nations and as men is how well prepared we are to meet these changes and, further, to use them for our health. ("The Creative Process")

It would appear that James Baldwin did not mature.

4 ✧✧✧

While Jimmy was alive, I made excuses for him, both to myself and in some of what I wrote about him. When he died, I wrote that I knew

the extent to which his life was a sacrifice to make white America take responsibility for its own evil instead of continuing to project it onto the souls of black folk. I knew his pain, his terror, his aloneness, and said to him once, "Jimmy, I really wonder if white people are worth the sacrifice of your life."

He threw up his hands in sad agreement and said, "But what else is one to do?"

I didn't know how to respond to him then, and now that he is dead, the answer, if there is one, will have to come from me.

Perhaps the day will come when white America will have made itself worthy of James Baldwin's sacrifice. But until that day, my grief will rage with the force of a thousand burning suns.

Well, the last sentence is certainly a bit of overripe prose and posturing of which I am ashamed. But it is not easy to be critical of Baldwin. I can still see myself, a college sophomore in 1957, reading *Notes of a Native Son,* not understanding much of its content but understanding through the mere presence of the book in my hand that it was permissible to be black and write with the lyricism of Shelley. And I needed to know that.

His work made a difference in the ways in which black and white were talked about in America, and a portion of his work is an act of love and faith of which America has not been worthy.

But there is the other side, the one that reveals a Baldwin who did not withstand the blinding light of a complex and multifarious human reality and instead settled for a chiaroscuro in which victims huddled in the cold shadows to face oppressors standing erect in the sunlight. But Baldwin's articulation of the race-as-victim expressed how the black collective saw and sees itself, which means that the Baldwin after *The Fire Next Time* did not present blacks with a vision of who they could become. He confirmed blacks in their excesses of self-pity and gave them permission not to take responsibility for who they were.

And then, there is the anti-Semitism. It is one of the great ironies of contemporary history that blacks insist on telling whites that they are incapable of understanding blacks or racism because they are not black and have not suffered racism. What, then, makes blacks think they know so much about Jews and understand anti-Semitism, or even have the capacity to recognize it? But today, anti-Semitism is often seen only as Hitlerian — a view that frees people to be content with the subtle anti-Semitism exemplified by James Baldwin.

There are two James Baldwins. The one who wrote until 1963 was stylistically brilliant, with a vision that penetrated to the essence of what it is to be human. The one after 1963 is, perhaps, an object lesson in what can happen to an artist who becomes the voice of a collective, and of that collective's worst tendencies. After 1963, his work no longer represents that of the intellectual taking risks. While there are always flashes of brilliance and insight, they are no longer connected to a coherent vision of the human condition.

In the last essay of *The Price of the Ticket*, there are these words:

> The object of one's hatred is never, alas, conveniently outside but is seated in one's lap, stirring in one's bowels and dictating the beat of one's heart. And if

one does not know this, one risks becoming an imitation — and, therefore, a continuation — of principles one imagines oneself to despise.

Let us be grateful for the wisdom of the early essays and take as a warning the latter part of Baldwin's career, which was, all too often, "an imitation" and "a continuation of principles" the early Baldwin taught us to despise.

Race

✧✧✧✧

"Black and White — Together"

✧✧✧

Only now do I begin to understand who we were and what that time was.

I was lecturing to the class I taught on the history of the civil-rights movement. It was a course I'd taught many times since 1973, and I was finding it increasingly difficult to teach because of the emotional pain that would surprise me while lecturing — a pain whose origins bewildered me.

I'd read about Holocaust survivors who only began remembering fifteen, twenty years after. But I was not that kind of survivor. The omnipresent threat of death on a Mississippi highway in 1964 was not Auschwitz. Yet, to live where the presence of death was as palpable as the smell of honeysuckle lacerated the soul in ways one dared not stop to know, in ways one could not know until a decade or two had passed.

That April night in 1988, I was telling the class about Fannie Lou Hamer, the soul incarnate of the civil-rights movement in Mississippi. She had been a sharecropper and was evicted from the plantation for attempting to register to vote. She moved into a small white frame house in

Ruleville and became the embodiment of freedom, not only for the blacks of Mississippi but for those of us much younger and more educated who had come to Mississippi to work for freedom.

The first time I was at her house, she showed me the holes in the walls from bullets fired in the night, aimed at her. She had a loaded rifle in each corner of every room.

When I started telling the class about the beating she received in the jail in Winona, Mississippi, pain stopped the words in my throat. I opened my mouth but words would not come. I waited but the words could not find their way past the tears, and finally, unable to speak, I cried. I did not know if the 175 students in the class were old enough not to be embarrassed by tears, but I was helpless to stop them.

Finally, my voice weak, cracking, hesitant, I told them how Mrs. Hamer was beaten in that jail, how they raised her dress and beat her between her legs, how they beat her and beat her, and how she had to come to New York periodically to be treated for the injuries from that beating, and how some of us believed her death was traceable to that beating.

But I wasn't crying for Mrs. Hamer that night, though it was convenient to let the class think so. My tears were for then and now, and for me, like darkness, in the chasm between the two.

✧✧✧

It is almost impossible to describe that world the civil-rights movement destroyed, that world of my childhood and adolescence ruled by signs decreeing where I was and was not allowed to go, what door I had to enter at the bus station and train station, where I had to sit on the bus. How do I explain as normal something so wholly absurd?

How do I explain what it is to live with the absurd and pretend to its ordinariness without becoming insane? How do I explain that I cannot be sure that my sanity was not hopelessly compromised because I grew up in a world in which the insane was as ordinary as margarine?

That is what Hannah Arendt meant by her brilliant phrase "the banality of evil." Evil is not always charismatic, nor does it have to involve a Faustian deal with Satan. More often than not, I suspect, evil is as unromantic as chunky peanut butter.

Don and Nancy lived in Sewanee, Tennessee, where Don was a student at the University of the South, an elite private school. They were white southerners. Nancy and I met in the winter of 1961 at Highlander Folk School, where we both worked. She invited me to spend the weekend with her and her husband. What could be more ordinary than friends spending a weekend together? But in 1961, it was illegal in the state of Tennessee for blacks and whites to socialize. The three of us could be arrested.

We knew. We were afraid. And we had no alternative. We were friends and friends spent weekends together.

That is how history is made. Ordinary people decide to live differently than their parents. Ordinary people decide to assert their humanness instead of continuing to live in deference to a collective that denies it.

Friday night and all day Saturday, I stayed inside their apartment. If their landlord saw me, they could be evicted. Don might be expelled from school and he was to be graduated in May.

Late that afternoon, Nancy got angry. I was her friend, wasn't I? She wasn't ashamed of me. She was proud to have me as her friend. She wanted a pizza and she wanted me to walk with her to the pizzeria.

I did. We were too afraid to talk to each other and held

our breaths as the cars slowed at the sight of the Negro and the attractive white woman walking side by side. But we walked slowly, and on the way back, Nancy put her arm through mine.

Back inside the apartment, we started laughing, a giddy laughter that quickly became hysterical, a laughter we could not stop, a laughter that put us on the floor, tears rolling down our faces, a laughter that left us gasping for breath, clutching our midsections. Whenever we regained our breath, I would glance at her or she at me for laughter to seize us again.

We were too young to realize that our laughter was the release of fear, that our laughter was tinged with the insane. But how could it not be? We had walked down the street together and had not been arrested or killed. If jail or death could be the price of friendship, how could we not have been insane?

I remember Nancy when I am on a university campus and see the black students sitting together at tables in the cafeteria. I remember her when I listen to black students talk about racism on their campus, when I hear them talking of being isolated, of the need for more black students, faculty, and administrators on the campus so there will be more of a black community.

I listen and I do not understand. Many of them are students at schools that would not accept blacks when it was my time to attend college. They have opportunities of which I could not have dreamed. Yet, they are dissatisfied.

We did not know about racism in 1961, and that is fortunate. We didn't know that white people were racists. To tell the truth, we didn't even know about black people then. We were Negroes, or colored. Because we didn't know, we welcomed those whites who were willing to risk their lives to destroy segregation. We were amazed that such white people existed.

Or maybe we were kinder then. We knew when whites were acting superior, when they were being paternalistic, when they were being racist (though we did not know the word), but we did not blame them. Neither they nor we had created the history we were trying to change. Their bodies on a lunch-counter stool at a sit-in, on a bus during the freedom rides, their talking to people on the dusty backroads of Mississippi, Alabama, and Georgia about registering to vote — these were sufficient proof of the quality of their souls. So what if his vocabulary or her personality needed a little work? Eating grits and fatback for breakfast and washing up every morning in cold water from a hydrant in the backyard helped one learn humility and humanity.

The Movement. It was a special time, a time when idealism was as palpable and delicious as a gentle summer rain, a time when freedom and love and justice seemed as immediate as ripe oranges shining seductively from a tree in one's yard. It was a time when we believed that the ideals of democracy would, at long last, gleam like endless, amber, waving fields of grain from the hearts and souls of every American. It was a time when we believed that love was a mighty stream that could purify the soul of a nation; and once purified, the nation would study war no more. We had a vision of a new world about to be born, and the vision burned us with a burning heat.

The Movement. It was singing "We Shall Overcome," arms crossed, hands holding those on either side; singing "Black and white together," the very sentiment unprecedented in American history; and singing loudly and holding a white hand or black one in yours, you were not only making history, you were History.

The Movement. It was the terror and loneliness of southern highways, where pine trees bordered the roads like tombstones. It was a time when going to jail was a badge of honor and respectability. It was cattle prods on exposed flesh; the hollow sound of billy clubs against skulls; bombed churches and four dead girls in Birmingham, Alabama; and it was death by bullets in the night, black and white together, martyred and mourned.

The Movement. It was idealism incarnate, the Word of nonviolence made Flesh, the willingness of the Flesh to be lacerated, to suffer, and even to be vanquished because more important than life was the inner knowledge that the "beloved community" could be made manifest. Then the inherent equality of all would be the standard of the body politic — for real.

In its beginnings in the latter half of the fifties, the Movement challenged us to sing the Lord's song in a strange land — a land in which we all sat by the rivers of Babylon and wept, though only a few knew they were weeping. In Montgomery, Alabama, Martin Luther King, Jr., was saying that yes, segregation was wrong, but one was not justified in destroying it by any means necessary. "All life is interrelated. All humanity is involved in a single process, and to the degree that I harm my brother, to that extent I am harming myself." We must be careful, he continued, not to do those things that will "intensify the existence of evil in the universe."

From a monastery in Kentucky, a monk named Thomas Merton was writing essays and books imbued with a clarity and authenticity unlike anything many of us had ever read.

> . . . our job is to love others without stopping to inquire whether or not they are worthy. That is not our business and, in fact, it is nobody's business. What we are asked to do is to love; and this love itself will render both ourselves and our neighbors worthy if anything can.

In California, in a place with the romantic name of North Beach, there came the voices of Allen Ginsberg, Jack Kerouac, Alan Watts, and Gary Snyder stripping the Eisenhower-and-McCarthy years of their gray-flanneled fear, and through their words we were invited to live life in all its fullness and blinding complexity. Henry Miller, the elder statesman of the Beat Generation, put it this way:

> I am not interested in the potential man. I am interested in what a man actualizes — or realizes — of his potential being. And what is the potential man, after all? Is he not the sum of all that is human? *Divine,* in other words? You think I am searching for God. I am not. God is. The world is. Man is. We are. The full reality, that's God — and man, and the world, and all that is, including the unnameable.

The Movement was not born from a desire to change the system. We wanted to move beyond systems.

In its early years, the Movement was a compelling force because political action was seen as a vehicle for spiritual expression. What really mattered were the values we lived by, the quality of who we were, and the subsequent quality of our relationships. Ending segregation was not the goal. (Anyone who thinks the aim of the early civil-rights movement was to sit down at a lunch counter next to a white person and eat a hamburger and drink a Coke insults not only the intelligence of blacks but our taste buds. We had always known that the food was better on our side of the tracks.) We wanted to create a new society based on feelings of community. To do that, the Movement had to be the paradigm of that new community.

Spring 1960. I stood in the student union building at Fisk University, staring at the bulletin board. The sit-in movement had begun in February in Greensboro, North

Carolina, had spread quickly to Nashville and other cities in the South, and had become national news. That spring afternoon of my senior year, I stood at the bulletin board and read the telegrams tacked there, telegrams expressing support of the sit-in movement from schools all over the country — Harvard, Yale, Stanford, the University of Chicago, Oberlin, and on and on and on.

I was bewildered. I had lived my twenty-one years shuddering within the lingering shadows of slavery. I had learned to walk great distances rather than sit in the back of segregated buses, to control my bodily functions so that I would not have to use segregated bathrooms, to go for hours in the southern heat rather than drink from the "Colored" fountains, and to choose hunger rather than buy food from segregated eating places.

Although I had lived with whites during a semester at San Diego State College my junior year, although I was close to white instructors at Fisk and had white friends among those who came on exchange to Fisk from schools such as Oberlin, Pomona, and Wooster, white people remained an implacable force as massive and undifferentiated as an iceberg. As I read those telegrams, I experienced that there were whites who cared, who did not think of segregation as a Negro problem (as we would have said then), but who knew it as it was — an American problem.

In the spring of 1961, a group of white college students established a new organization, Students for a Democratic Society. SDS condemned not only segregation but the hypocrisy of the nation that allowed it while continuing to call itself democratic. SDS asked fundamental questions about the values by which Americans lived.

The civil-rights movement and what came to be known as the New Left were parallel and overlapping forces for change, not only in how America conducted itself at home, but in what it did abroad — especially in a small country in Southeast Asia called Vietnam, where presidents Kennedy and Johnson were sending Americans to kill peasants and make the world safe for democracy.

By the midsixties, the Movement was not only blacks chanting "Freedom Now!" but a generation of disaffected white youths questioning and organizing against American involvement in Vietnam, and demanding fundamental changes in the content and structure of higher education. Other white youths, however, sought to change the face of America by removing themselves from it and "dropped out."

The Movement, then, was not only Martin Luther King, Jr., writing a letter from Birmingham jail, but Pete Seeger singing "We Shall Overcome" at Carnegie Hall, and Jefferson Airplane singing "White Rabbit" in Golden Gate Park. It was flowers placed in the rifle barrels of soldiers at the Pentagon antiwar demonstration in the fall of 1967, and it was burning draft cards. It was smoking cigarettes that enabled you to see through a glass darkly, or made you think you did. It was Tom Hayden, Mark Rudd, and Bernadine Dohrn; it was Tim Leary and Abbie Hoffman; it was underground newspapers and classic cartoons by R. Cobb. It was hair — not only the musical announcing the Age of Aquarius, but hair wreathing the face and flowing down the back, or, if you were black, crowning the head like an inverted bowl shaped from the strands of dreams.

Ultimately, it was too much, a time too big to grasp, or to understand, or even to know what it was you were experiencing. Events that shook you to the soul happened too often and too frequently: the assassinations of a president, that president's brother, Martin Luther King, Jr., Malcolm X — not to mention the martyrs of the civil-rights movement itself: Jimmie Lee Jackson, Viola Liuzzo, Jonathan Daniels, the Reverend James Reeb, James Chaney,

Andrew Goodman, Michael Schwerner, William Moore, and those killed in the riots of the long, hot summers.

We did not know America would extract such a price to maintain the status quo. We did not know the Justice Department of Robert Kennedy would not be eager to use the power of the federal government to protect civil-rights workers. We did not know that seeking the end of segregation and disenfranchisement would lead the liberal press to accuse us of wanting too much, too soon. Above all, perhaps, we did not know that the values we sought to embody — the values of nonviolence and the beloved community — were not the ones that America wanted for itself.

The decade that began with the singing of "We Shall Overcome" staggered to its end with shouts of "Burn, Baby, Burn!" That was too long and too arduous a journey to travel in a mere ten years. The decade that began with black and white together trying to create the beloved community ended with taunts of "Honky!" and cries of "Black Power!"

The most detailed catalog of the events of that time fails to convey its profuse complexity. A hundred flowers bloomed, but they were of different varieties, in unnameable colors, and had unidentifiable scents. The time was bigger than even its most well known actors and it was frightening to feel yourself being lived by History, to become a spectator in your own life.

I do not remember the first time I heard of Malcolm X, but I do know the first time I took him seriously. During the winter of 1963, I worked for the welfare department in Harlem. The month of February at the Harlem office was devoted to raising money for the NAACP. One morning my supervisor, who was white, informed me that the following day was our unit's turn to raise money and that he had scheduled me to sit at a table in the lobby from twelve to two and sell cookies. I told him I didn't support the N-double-A and had no intention of raising money for it. He looked at me coldly and said, "What are you? One of those followers of Malcolm X?" The way he said it told me all I needed to know and I returned his stare and said, "Yes." After that he treated me with cool but proper respect, something that had been missing. Such was the power of Malcolm X.

Malcolm derided integration and mocked nonviolence. He scorned love and extolled power. He had contempt for everything white and a startling love for everything black. What he said was hard to embrace. It was even harder to deny.

Most of us did not follow Malcolm, but what he said followed us like some nagging superego, especially after four girls were murdered in the bombing of the church in Birmingham. Was Malcolm right? Was violence the only response to violence?

One day in the midsixties — 1965, I think — I was in the Forty-second Street library and ran into a friend whose first words were an excited, "Have you read this yet?" He thrust into my hands a book called *The Wretched of the Earth* by Frantz Fanon.

Fanon gave us words by which to know ourselves anew. In his writings we found the term *Third World,* and no longer would we identify ourselves as American. He told us that we were a colonized people, which gave us a political identity and aligned us with all the struggles of the twentieth century against colonialism. Most important, Fanon told us that violence was redemptive, that violence was the only means by which the colonized could cleanse themselves of the violence of the colonizers.

We did not have to wonder about the violence of the

colonizers, because every night on the news we saw US soldiers carrying out a war in a country we had never heard of. The nation was at war and something happened that was perhaps unprecedented in American history: a significant number of young Americans sided openly with the enemy. Young men fled to Canada and Sweden rather than be drafted to fight an unjust war. Draft cards and American flags were burned at antiwar rallies and Phil Ochs sang "I Ain't A-Marching Anymore."

At the same historical moment, the predominantly black civil-rights movement and the predominantly white anti–Vietnam War movement became anti-American. Suddenly, America was the enemy.

Common sense should have told us that it is impossible to transform a nation if you hate it. But that is one of the dangers of idealism. When it is let loose in the public arena, it is like an animal in heat and in desperate need of a sexual joining. All too quickly, unrequited idealism can become surly and aggressive. All too quickly, unrequited idealism becomes rage, bares the teeth that have been lurking behind the smile as pretty as a morning glory, and, enraged, bites itself, never feeling the pain or knowing that the blood staining its teeth is its own.

But the signs had been there almost from the beginning. I remember hearing the chant "Freedom Now! Freedom Now!" and being afraid of what would happen if we didn't get "freedom now." Later in the sixties, Jim Morrison of the Doors shouted, "We want the world and we want it now!" We should have been frightened that such infantilism had become a political norm. We weren't, and that should have frightened us even more.

Freedom did not come now. We didn't get the world — at least not warm from the oven, as light and flaky as a croissant. Because freedom did not come now, because we did not get the world, we turned against the nation we had wanted to love, a nation that did not want our love. Or so it seemed.

And we turned against each other.

Spring 1968. I am sitting in my apartment in New York with a close Movement friend. I am a very private person, and there are not many with whom I share my home and family. He is one of the few who have eaten in my home and played with my children. We are alone that afternoon, chatting with unguarded ease. Then, apropos of nothing, he says: "I probably shouldn't say this, man, but I don't think you should be married to a white woman. You probably think it's none of my business." Quietly, I responded, "You're right." He nods and there is nothing more to be said — about that or anything else. After a moment of silence as long as winter, he gets up. "Take care of yourself," he says. "Yeah, you, too," I respond. I never saw him again, and a few years later he was dead, killed in a bombing.

But over the next few years, as I spoke on college campuses around the nation, I found myself being asked, repeatedly and angrily, to explain how I could consider myself black and have a white wife. For a while, I wondered, too.

But having grown up in the South, where whites decreed whom I could and could not marry, I was not going to turn around and give blacks power over the most personal of choices. That blacks wanted and sought to take such power was only a sign of the times, however.

Both the black and the white movements attacked individuals, for the personal had become political, and the gray-flanneled conformity of the fifties was replaced by a blue-jeaned and Afroed totalitarianism.

A mysterious and mystical entity called "the people"

became the standard against which everyone was measured and judged. Your actions, thoughts, and lifestyle had
to serve the needs of "the people." At one meeting, I asked
a simple question, "Which people? Do you mean the junk-
ies, winos, and prostitutes? Do you mean the churchgoing
people, the manual laborers, the unwed mothers, or the
strivers?" When the meeting continued as if I had not spoken, I knew that I had committed a revolutionary faux
pas. I also knew I had asked a good question.

Wasn't the role of the intellectual simply that — to ask
good questions? But an intellectual could not do that if he
or she felt guilty about being an intellectual, if she or he
found virtue only in something called "the working class"
or something even more amorphous called "the people."

In his very fine novel *An Admirable Woman*, the late
Arthur Cohen's heroine says these words:

> The mind has its work and its materials; it has no
> choice in this respect. It can do nothing else but work
> properly — balancing thrust with caution, intuition
> with verification, argument with detail, interpreta-
> tion with groundwork, grand truth with the webbing
> of subtle argument. The working of mind is a slow
> and patient procedure. It cannot be rushed. . . . Clar-
> ity is the moral luster of the mind.

This was our birthright as intellectuals. To possess it,
we needed to withstand the terror and loneliness and isolation inherent in being an intellectual. By definition, the
intellectual must be an outsider, because only from the
outside can one see inside. We succumbed to that under-
standable human need to be at the party and stand beside
the fireplace, drinking hot cider.

That was predictable, because it is only a short step
from idealism to ideology. Both hold out the promise of

giving a life meaning; both promise to shelter us from the uncertainties and anxieties of self-knowledge.

Ideology does not permit self-doubt and questioning, because it is a cosmology that answers all questions, past, present, and future. Eventually, thought becomes unnecessary, and the struggle to be human is scorned as individualism. We cease to be human and become impervious archetypes. The factionalism and political name-calling that had alienated so many from the Old Left became the language of the black movement and the New Left.

In the spring of 1969, SDS passed a resolution asserting the Black Panther party as the "vanguard" of the black movement, the true representatives of revolutionary nationalism. In my weekly column in *The Guardian,* I objected and wrote, in part: "By presuming to know what program, ideology, military strategy, and what particular organizations best serve the interests of the black community," SDS was being "more white than revolutionary."

The Guardian published a response by Kathleen Cleaver, the Panther secretary of communications. Among other things, she called me a "counter-revolutionary," "a fool" peddling "madness," and a "racist" before she ended with these eloquent words: "Fuck Julius Lester. All power to the people!"

I remembered Kathleen from when she had come to work in the Atlanta SNCC office: a young woman with a big grin and a lot of enthusiasm. We were pals, in the best sense of that word, able to laugh and play together.

What had happened to her? What was happening to us all? Why did Kathleen need me to agree with her? Why did blacks need me to leave my wife so they could be black? When the personal becomes political, persons cease to exist. When persons cease to exist, war is imminent.

I was not surprised to hear rumors that the Panthers

were going to kill me. I believed the rumors because I knew people whom the Panthers had threatened at gunpoint over political differences.

The rumors were only rumors, but what did it mean that I had more space and freedom to think and write in Nixon's America than in the Movement with all its revolutionary rhetoric?

In September of the same year, Ho Chi Minh died. I had been in North Vietnam for a month in 1967 and had witnessed US bombing raids at a time when the government was still denying them. Most of all, though, I remembered the lyrical beauty of that country. Perhaps that is why my response to Ho's death was to write a poem and publish it as my weekly column in *The Guardian*.

> Half awakened by the light of morning
> choking in the greyness
> of a third of September Wednesday,
> I reached out for the
> roundness
> softness
> fullness
> allness of her
> and she, awakened,
> began to move,
> softly,
> silently,
> gently,
> and my hand found that place,
> that hidden place,
> that secret place,
> that
> won-
> der-

ful place
and in the quiescent light of
a third of September Wednesday morning,
I felt my penis being taken into the
salty
thick
fluidity
of her swirling movement
easily
softly
gently
(as the children were waking).

Afterwards,
my penis, moist and warm,
resting on my thigh like some
fish washed onto the beach by full moontide,
I turned on the radio
and we heard that
Ho Chi Minh lay dying.

(The fog covered the seagulls that
sit on the rocky beach when the tide is out.)

I retreated from her,
not talking that day as the radio told me
(every hour on the hour)
that Ho Chi Minh lay dying.

Finally, when night had covered the fog,
we heard that
Ho Chi Minh was dead
and I came back to her.
Ho Chi Minh was dead.
I wanted her again.
The softness
the roundness

the fullness
the allness.

Ho Chi Minh was dead.

When the next issue of *The Guardian* came out, a poem
of Ho's was in the space where my column always appeared. Angry, I called the office wanting to know why my
poem had not been published. The editor told me the staff
had decided that my poem would not be understood as the
appreciation of Ho that it was if it were published the
week of Ho's death. They had decided to delay publication
for a week. I asked why they hadn't let me know, or discussed it with me. The editor said they had been too busy.

The poem was published the following week; and the
week after, my final column appeared, announcing my resignation from the paper.

I had thought that the revolution would create a society
in which power elites did not arbitrarily determine what
"the people" might and might not understand. I should
have known that the revolution wouldn't be erotic.

I left *The Guardian,* but it was hard to leave the Movement. It had been identity and life, family and community.
When Dave Dellinger's magazine, *Liberation,* asked me to
write for it, I agreed. Less than a year passed, and once
again I wrote something that a Movement publication did
not want to publish.

The occasion was the trial in New Haven of seven
members of the Black Panther party who had been accused of torturing and murdering Alex Rackley, another
Panther. Three party members admitted their active partic-
ipation in the torture and murder of Rackley. Yet, black
and white radicals were demonstrating on the New Haven
Green and many articles were published in the radical
press demanding that the New Haven Seven be freed. The

rationale? It was impossible for blacks to receive justice in America. White sycophancy toward the black movement was setting a new standard for madness. I sat down at the typewriter.

> ... we can self-righteously cite the verdict of the Nuremberg Trials when we want to condemn the military establishment and the politicians. We can say to them that you are personally responsible for what you do, that you do not have to follow orders and there are no extenuating circumstances. Yet, we can turn right around and become Adolf Eichmanns, eloquent apologists for the Movement's My Lai. . . . our morality is used to condemn others, but it is not to be applied to ourselves. We can react with outrage when four are murdered at Kent State, but when a professor is killed in the dynamiting of the Mathematics Building at the University of Wisconsin, we don't give it a second thought. When they kill, it's murder. When we kill, there are extenuating circumstances. It was an accident, we say. The blast went off too soon.
>
> The murder of Alex Rackley was . . . the logical culmination of the politics we have been espousing, a politics of violence-for-the-sake-of-violence, a politics which too quickly and too neatly divides people into categories of "revolutionary" and "counterrevolutionary." The murder of Alex Rackley is the result of a politics which more and more begins to resemble the politics which we are supposedly seeking to displace.

The editors of *Liberation* held the article for three months. Finally, I had a tense meeting with them in which they argued that the prosecution could use my article against the Panthers. Did I want that? I was asked. How many times during my years in the Movement had someone tried to control my thoughts, my words, or my deeds — even whom I would love — by saying that such-and-such would not be in the best interests of "the people"; that such-and-such would merely play into the hands of the "enemy"; that I was being individualistic, and that people in the Movement had to submit to discipline, and that my thoughts and life were not more important than "the people."

I knew only that as a writer and an intellectual, my responsibility was to that minuscule portion of the truth that came into my keeping. As a person, my responsibility was to be as fully human as I could. Giving your soul to ideology permitted you to rationalize murder, to attack friends, to deny the power and beauty of the erotic. Allegiance to ideology gave you permission to turn other human beings into abstractions — and as a black kid growing up under segregation in the forties and fifties, I knew what that felt like because, dear God, my soul still bled from the wounds. If I had learned nothing else, I had learned that you do not turn another human being into an abstraction without becoming an abstraction to yourself, and that to turn another person into an abstraction is murder. And whether murder is justified in the name of God, freedom, justice, socialism, revolution, or democracy, it is still murder.

Liberation published the article, but I left the Movement. It had ceased to be anything I recognized or wanted to be a part of.

Only now do I begin to understand how revolutionary those early years were, those years of "black and white together." Only now, when I see black and white more separated than they were in the segregated South of my youth — only now do I recognize that that brief period from 1960 to 1968 was the only time in American history when blacks and whites came together to know each other, not only as blacks and whites, but as persons, too.

It has been forgotten that the civil-rights movement was not a black movement. The leadership was, in the main, black; most of its participants were black. But not all. By no means all. The civil-rights movement was more integrated than anything has ever been in American history. Whites, too, risked their lives, and whites died, and no one wants to remember.

Those who want to see the civil-rights movement as merely political are mistaken. Segregation had to be destroyed; the right of blacks to vote had to be affirmed and ensured. But that was not the Movement's object. We wanted to change the ways people related to each other. All those who were murdered, all those who were jailed, all those who were beaten, all those whose psyches still bear wounds from having stared death in the eye once too often did not suffer just so Jesse Jackson could run for president.

But what happened was, perhaps, inevitable. Idealism touches the young, bestowing golden visions of what can be; but it is in the nature of the young to be impatient, and when the gold of the vision does not fall upon the earth in a shimmering drizzle, the young become angry — and idealism denied is dangerous.

Idealism was replaced by ideology. The dream was replaced by doctrine. Feeling was replaced by concept. Ideology does not care about individuals. It cares only for itself. It demands that a person submit to its doctrines, and so, the ideology of blackness took its place alongside the much older ideology of whiteness. I see black students on campuses separating themselves from white students and I want to scream: "No! Blackness will not save you, just as whiteness has not saved them. Nothing will save you except that you love yourselves enough as persons to risk loving *them,* especially because they may not deserve it."

But does any of us *deserve* love? Isn't love always a gift of which we try to be worthy? And how can we be worthy if we do not risk making a part of us the pain and suffering of another. That is the only means through which I can comprehend the other's humanity. Trust between persons is established when each is receptive to the abiding sorrows of the other.

Ideologies are attempts to make sense of the world. We delude ourselves when we use them to seek our identity, when we wear them and think we know who we are. Identity cannot be resolved so easily, so simply.

Ultimately, the task is to be utterly human. Only to the extent that I know and accept my utter humanity will I be able to see others as they are, as nothing more than and nothing less than utterly human. When we are able to do this, we will have moved beyond ideology into terror — and then, only then, will we be free.

❖❖❖

Maybe I started crying when I remembered Mrs. Hamer because I was weary of being beaten, weary of being assaulted by black anger when I wrote critically about black anti-Semitism or Jesse Jackson. Did William Moore, the Reverend James Reeb, Michael Schwerner, Andrew Goodman, Jonathan Daniels, and all the others die just so blacks could become a concept to themselves?

Maybe I cried because I had not wanted to live with death as palpable as sunshine on Mississippi roads and I did not feel like a hero because I had. It hurt to live with death. It still does.

Maybe I cried because to live in the chasm between then and now, to live and try to pull then into now is a task greater than I am. Maybe I cried because then was then and now is now and that is how it should be and I hate that.

At the next class, a black female student gave me a card and said, "Thank you." Another black woman student brought me flowers and said nothing. And I thought I felt a barely perceptible movement somewhere in the universe, and I dared hope that then had moved a little closer to now.

Blacks and the Immigrant Experience

✧✧✧

In 1956 — I was seventeen — the Soviet Union suppressed an uprising in Hungary against the Communist government there. I recall the newspaper photographs of Hungarians throwing rocks and bottles at Russian tanks, and I remember hearing these men and women referred to by the media as "freedom fighters."

Regardless of how ardently one desires freedom, a rock is no threat to a tank. The Hungarian "freedom fighters" were subdued. The United States opened the gates of immigration to those fleeing political persecution and the media carried moving stories of men and women coming to America for the freedom denied them in Hungary.

One evening, after watching one such story on television, my father said bitterly: "Look at them! They can barely speak English and they get a better welcome in this country than we do, and we've been here longer than almost anybody. People are falling all over themselves to give those Hungarians jobs and a place to live, and if a black man walked in and tried to get the same job and buy the same house, they'd tell him no."

148

My father's bitterness was not the product of frustrated dreams and unrealized aspirations. I did not grow up in some stereotypical ghetto where poverty and hopelessness reign like royalty. My father was a minister and we were comfortably and securely middle-class. My father drove a Cadillac, and if I wore blue jeans much of the time, that was by choice. My father's ungenerous response to the Hungarian refugees emanated from something deeper than the economic circumstances of his life.

In the spring of 1959, I was attending San Diego State College in California, and while walking across campus one afternoon, I was stopped by a white friend.

"Julius, I want you to meet one of our Hungarian friends," she said, gesturing to the young man standing next to her. Having been raised to regard politeness as an art form second only to ballet, I smiled, shook the young man's hand, chatted pleasantly with him for a few moments, and then walked away so angry that I never spoke to my friend again.

If I had not been so rationally polite, I would have said, "No Hungarian is a friend of mine." But that would have been gratuitously cruel to someone who had done nothing to me. Neither would it have reflected the totality of my response, for there was also a part of me that was proud that America opened its borders to refugees from political persecution, that America offered the opportunity for life to so many who faced living deaths at best, and actual deaths at worst.

My rage was at my white friend, who was so ignorant and so innocent that she refused to know that my attitudes and responses to immigrants could not be wholly the same as hers.

To understand the black response to the immigrant experience, rage is the necessary place of beginning, but it is no more than that. Rage is a mask hiding deeper and more painful emotions, emotions that even the one suffering the rage wants to keep hidden.

The summer of 1986 saw the observance of the one-hundredth birthday of the Statue of Liberty. It was a time of national celebration. Newspapers and television carried stories and interviews with immigrants recounting their coming to America, their thoughts and emotions on first seeing the statue. How painful it was to read and listen to such stories; how maddening to listen to immigrants express with deep sincerity and in tears how much they loved America, how America had given them opportunities they would not have had otherwise.

I remembered the opening lines of a poem by James M. Whitfield, a nineteenth-century black poet.

> America, it is to thee,
> Thou boasted land of liberty, —
> It is to thee I raise my song,
> Thou land of blood and crime and wrong.

I could not watch the televised Fourth-of-July festivities for very long and when I saw photographs of fireworks exploding around the illuminated Statue of Liberty, I was dismayed that the nation could so celebrate itself and not know that its celebration was a rebuke and an insult to that 10 percent of its population which had its beginnings in the killing arrogance of white people who thought they had divine sanction to steal other human beings by force, to enslave them, use them for their own aggrandizement and profit, and sell them or kill them when they refused to be so used.

America had a birthday party, but I could not attend; and America did not notice my absence, which means it did not care that I was not present.

In 1852, Frederick Douglass was invited to speak at a

Fourth-of-July celebration in Rochester, New York, and
his words have lost none of their truth.

> Fellow-citizens, pardon me, allow me to ask, why am
> I called upon to speak here today? What have I, or
> those I represent, to do with your national indepen-
> dence? Are the great principles of political freedom
> and of natural justice, embodied in the Declaration
> of Independence, extended to us? and am I, there-
> fore, called upon to bring our humble offering to the
> national altar, and to confess the benefits and express
> devout gratitude for the blessings resulting from your
> independence to us?
>   Would to God, both for your sakes and ours, that
> an affirmative answer could be truthfully returned to
> these questions!
>   . . . But such is not the case. . . . I am not included
> within the pale of this glorious anniversary! . . . The
> blessings in which you, this day, rejoice, are not en-
> joyed in common. The rich inheritance of justice, lib-
> erty, prosperity and independence, bequeathed by
> your fathers, is shared by you, not by me. The sun-
> light that brought light and healing to you, has
> brought stripes and death to me. This Fourth of July
> is *yours,* not *mine. You* may rejoice, *I* must mourn.
> To drag a man in fetters into the grand illuminated
> temple of liberty, and call upon him to join you in
> joyous anthems, were inhuman mockery and sacrile-
> gious irony. Do you mean, citizens, to mock me, by
> asking me to speak today? . . .
>   What . . . is your 4th of July? . . . your celebration
> is a sham; your boasted liberty, an unholy license;
> your national greatness, swelling vanity; your sounds
> of rejoicing are empty and heartless; your denuncia-
> tion of tyrants, brass fronted impudence; your shouts

of liberty and equality, hollow mockery; your prayers and hymns, your sermons and thanksgivings, with all your religious parade and solemnity, are, to Him, mere bombast, fraud, deception, impiety, and hypocrisy — a thin veil to cover up crimes which would disgrace a nation of savages. . . .

Yes, there is rage in Douglass's words, but grief and tears are there also because he feared that whites would respond by turning away from black anguish.

That is my fear. I do not begrudge the immigrants their experience of America as the shelter in a world of storms. America is unique because no other country has so consistently and so generously opened its borders to people from all over the world. I would not want it to be otherwise. But what prevents me from wholeheartedly celebrating this extraordinary attribute of the American character is that the immigrant advance into American life and culture has been at the expense of those of us who were in America one year before the Pilgrims arrived at Plymouth Rock.

How often have I been talking with a nonblack and had that person say: "My grandparents got off the boat at Ellis Island and had nothing. They succeeded in America. They were discriminated against. They were poor, but they worked hard and they made it. Why haven't blacks done the same?"

This attitude reflects not only a blissful and willful ignorance of history, but one bereft of that generosity of spirit that would make us one nation instead of a nation more and more racially divided.

The immigrants and the children and grandchildren of immigrants who carry such an attitude conveniently overlook some painful facts of history. One was alluded to by my father during the time of the Hungarian uprising. Nonblack immigrants were given jobs from which blacks were excluded. For all the glory in the history of the union movement, one of its inglorious chapters was its systematic exclusion of blacks. Thus, an immigrant could get off a boat at Ellis Island knowing no English, yet economic opportunity existed for him or her that did not exist for blacks who were born citizens.

Elsewhere in that Fourth-of-July address, Frederick Douglass made a simple statement: "Oppression makes a wise man mad." He did not mean angry. There is a place at which the immigrant experience and the black experience meet and blacks teeter on the edge of madness because their own invisibility in American eyes only increases. How can it not when waves and waves of immigrants land on the American shore, procure jobs denied to blacks, and then, as if to prove their Americanness, become racists.

Blacks look at immigrants arriving in America and do not see refugees from political persecution. We see people who are going to take jobs from a black community that is already reeling under an unemployment rate of over 40 percent. We see, too, people who are potential racists. (We thought America had grown enough of its own without having to import more.)

Some years ago, at the conclusion of a panel discussion on affirmative action at an elite private college, a young white man, his blond hair shining like sunlight on a knight's helmet, addressed me coldly and said, "My grandfather was an immigrant from Switzerland. He had nothing to do with racism in America."

I looked at the young man and said, with equal coldness, "His skin was white, wasn't it?"

The young man did not understand, and I will go further and say that he willfully refused to understand. I did not question that the young man's grandfather was a decent and caring human being, but in a society where the value of goodness is conferred on whiteness, it is an economic and social and political advantage to be white. White skin carries privileges that America acknowledges and rewards. Black skin is a liability that is penalized and punished. And I say that as a black who is successful far beyond anything my father could have dreamed.

Regardless of how successful I might become, I can never feel for America what the immigrant feels. America is not a shelter in a storm for us. America is the storm. The least a nation is supposed to give a citizen is the unquestioned knowledge that he or she is valued by the nation. America has never wavered in its message to its black citizens: your value to the nation is less than that of white citizens.

How else am I to interpret the fact that black children are twice as likely to die during the first year of life as white children, twice as likely to have no regular source of medical care, and 25 percent more likely to die from illness during childhood? How else am I to interpret the fact that black children are placed in classes for educable mentally retarded children at three times the rate of white children? How else am I to understand that 49 percent of black women with breast cancer survive as opposed to 68 percent of white women? How am I supposed to believe that America, this nation of immigrants, cares about black life when four times as many black women die in childbirth as white women? How can I truly love America when I know that whites can expect to live 6.1 years longer than blacks?

The simple fact is that in its beginnings, America conceived of itself as a nation of and for white people, and European immigrants have been included within that definition. I know European immigrants did not find the streets of America paved with gold, that Italians and Irish and Poles were discriminated against, that prejudice continues to exist against immigrant groups. But prejudice against immigrants did not organize itself into institutional racism — an institutional racism that immigrants were a part of, because their skins were white. Until immigrants and their descendants feel in the sinew of their souls that there is a qualitative difference in the tears that come to their eyes when they see the American flag and the tears that come to mine when I do, there is no possibility that black and white Americans will have a chance of communicating with each other; and if we cannot communicate with each other, we will only continue to move further and further apart, until we have nothing in common except enmity.

During the festivities on that July 4, 1986, I happened to turn on the television when President Reagan was speaking. I have lived long enough not to expect eloquence or intelligence from an American president, but I could not help hoping that the president would acknowlege that while it was right and proper for America to celebrate the one-hundredth birthday of the Statue of Liberty and all it has meant as a symbol of hope, it was also right and proper for America to acknowledge that the statue has not been that for black Americans.

I would have liked the president to apologize to black Americans on behalf of all the immigrants and their descendants, of whom he is one, for the fact that that beacon of liberty has not shone her torch on blacks, and that, as painful as it is to acknowledge, immigrants owe some of their success to the fact that one of the rungs on their climb up the ladder of success was the backs of black people. I wanted the president to make it clear that he was speaking in the generality, that he was speaking not about individual immigrants — some of whom, certainly, did all they could within the contexts of their lives to alleviate racism and prejudice — but, rather, about the forces in American life that allow racism to flourish like vegetation in a rain forest. I would've liked it very much if the president had gone on to reveal that he felt black suffering and had made it a part of him, for we are not bound together as human beings because we all succeed. We do not, and that is an unchangeable part of how things are. What binds us together as human beings is that we all suffer, and the suffering that has brought immigrants to America as a refuge from suffering should have made them empathic with the suffering of blacks and generous toward them. What is so painful, what is almost unforgivable, is how ready immigrants and their descendants have been to add to black suffering.

I would have been especially moved if the president had also acknowledged the original inhabitants of his land and their brutal displacement and degradation, which have been enshrined in American history as the "winning of the West." What this nation of immigrants did to native Americans cannot be undone, but there must be a public acknowledgment of what was done and a public asking of forgiveness for the fact that this nation created itself by destroying the people who were already here.

If the president could've made such a speech, it would've meant that America had, at long last, matured into a nation that accepted responsibility for all of its history rather than seizing on a portion and glorifying it as the whole. America has a large and frightening shadow that it refuses to look at and refuses to claim as its own. Until America claims that shadow as its own, we will continue to be a nation of children forever claiming that we have done nothing wrong and that all the wrongs that have been done — well, they just kind of happened and we don't know how. Black people know that the wrongs didn't just happen.

At the conclusion of the president's speech at the Statue of Liberty, he pushed a button that began the fireworks display. I wished he could've pushed another button, one that would've made the Statue of Liberty turn around, for the Lady in the Harbor has its back to America.

It is time for the Statue of Liberty to turn its face, its upraised arm, toward America and to allow the radiance of that torch, with all its promise and hope, to shine on America's black citizens. Perhaps, then, when America celebrates the Lady's two-hundredth birthday, one of my descendants can celebrate as I was not able to wholly celebrate the anniversary of her first century.

Farrakhan

✧✧✧

As a religious and political figure, Louis Farrakhan is not singular or unique. He is merely the black representative in a worldwide resurgence of religious fundamentalism that includes Shiite Muslims in the Middle East, Meir Kahane and much of the Orthodox rabbinate in Israel and America, Pope John Paul II in the Vatican, and Pat Robertson and Jerry Falwell in white America.

What they have in common are (1) their literal interpretation of their respective scriptures, (2) their use of religion as a political force, and (3) their articulation of what they consider traditional values, values they want governments to endorse and codify as civil law — that is, their shared belief in theocracy. It is apparent to them that civil law has failed in controlling the behavior of citizens. Therefore, they argue, religious precepts must be encoded in law if society is not to fall into chaos.

Religious fundamentalists share a concept of society that is, at base, antidemocratic in the sense that diversity of political expression and lifestyle is condemned. That Robertson is willing to include Jews in his vision of society and Farrakhan isn't does not endear Robertson, because, like Farrakhan, he believes that his religious beliefs are synonymous with universal truth.

The religious fundamentalism of the eighties was a reaction against the religious liberalism of the sixties. Pat Robertson came in answer to Father Daniel Berrigan, the Reverend William Sloane Coffin, and Rabbi Abraham Joshua Heschel. Louis Farrakhan is the answer to Martin Luther King, Jr. Those liberals who now feel threatened by religious fundamentalism in the political arena did not feel threatened when rabbis and ministers marched for civil rights and protested against the Vietnam War. Because they did not raise questions about the meaning of the clergy in politics when they agreed with the politics, it behooves them to be cautious now that there are ministers and rabbis in the political arena espousing a politics they do not like.

What is at issue are the values Americans live by. Despite Farrakhan's rhetoric and tone, the values of the Nation of Islam are staunchly conservative. Look at any picture of Farrakhan. His face gleams as if his mother had just scrubbed him with Ivory soap. His hair is cut short and looks as if it had been slicked down with a hundred vigorous strokes of a brush. He wears a suit, white shirt, and bow tie. I scare more white people walking through airports with my black cowboy hat on than Farrakhan would.

For thirty years now, the Nation of Islam has been attempting to inject values of responsibility and stability into poor black communities, values as American as Scotch tape. Farrakhan and the religious right espouse the values Norman Rockwell depicted on the covers of *The Saturday Evening Post*.

Farrakhan's basic political conservatism gives him a symbolic stature in black America; that is, his values are familiar and safe. This is why educated blacks say in all sincerity that no one in the black community takes Farrakhan's anti-Semitism seriously. It, too, is symbolic of black America's alienation from the mainstream.

The value put on symbolic expression by blacks reflects the degree to which black America feels politically impotent, despite the number of black political officials. Thus, Farrakhan's politics are secondary to his embodiment of black aspirations to be respected and perceived as powerful — that is, to be seen as no different from whites.

Anti-Semitism is more than symbolic expression. To emphasize its symbolic dimension and ignore its pathological one is to overlook that anti-Semitism has been a part of black American history for a long while.

The black folktale that follows is from Zora Neale Hurston's *Mules and Men,* a collection of stories gathered in Florida in the 1930s. The tale is much older than that and probably dates back to the 1870s.

When God created people, He didn't give them their souls. God knew that the soul was very powerful and he wanted to wait until people were strong enough to hold their souls in their bodies. God kept the soul beneath the skirts of his garment and one day, a white man walked past God and just as he did, a little breeze lifted up the hem of God's skirt and some light from the soul streamed out and it was so bright that the white man got scared and ran away. Next day, a black man was walking past God and he got curious about the soul, so he went over and tried to peek under God's skirt and the light and warmth from the soul was so powerful that it knocked him over and he ran away. A few days later, along came the Jew. He was walking past God when a big wind came and lifted up God's skirt. The Jew saw the soul gleaming brightly and streaming with lights of many colors and he ran and grabbed the soul. Well, the soul was so powerful that it knocked the Jew down and rolled him over and over on the ground. But the Jew wouldn't let go. That soul knocked him up in the sky and back down on the ground, but the Jew still wouldn't let go. The Jew hugged the soul so hard that it broke into a lot of little pieces. The white man and the black man came and picked up the little pieces and put them inside and that's how man got his soul. But one of these days, God is going to make the Jew divide that soul up fair so everybody gets equal amounts.

Perhaps it is not coincidence that around the time Hurston collected this tale in Florida, a man named Elijah Poole, later known as Elijah Muhammad, started the Nation of Islam.

The basic mythology of the Nation of Islam is that the original humans were black, and that blacks were the Chosen People. But a mad scientist by the name of Yacub grafted an evil white people from the skin of blacks and the first evil whites he grafted were — you guessed it — Jews.

The anti-Semitism Farrakhan espouses is central to the Nation of Islam. He seeks to replace Jews as the Chosen People with blacks. This is not new. There are small groups of black Hebrews who consider themselves to be the "true" Jews chosen by God and who see all other Jews as imposters. Both Christians and Muslims have presented themselves as the new people chosen by God to replace Jews.

The anti-Semitism of the Nation of Islam took political form during Elijah Muhammad's life, manifesting itself in attacks against Israel and Zionism. There was an occa-

sional anti-Semitic remark in the speeches of Malcolm X,
but not until Louis Farrakhan did the anti-Semitism come
to the forefront.

Why? For the answer, one must go back to the black-
consciousness movement of the latter sixties, when many
American blacks began identifying with the Third World,
and in particular with Africa and the Arab world. Such
identification was not merely a political stance. In the process of rediscovering the African homeland, they learned
that Islam is a dominant religion in black Africa. Although
there were not then many blacks in the United States who
adhered to and practiced Islam, they were sympathetic to
it as a symbol of black identity. They were also sympathetic to it as way of repudiating white Western values.
From those came the African slave trade and slavery, racism, and discrimination. Western values, and Jews are included in that, have denied the integrity and sacredness of
black existence. Islam was seen as the antithesis of whiteness and the West, and identification with Islam brought
blacks into an identification with the Arab nations and,
consequently, with religious and political anti-Semitism.

Farrakhan's religious fundamentalism is, therefore, typ-
ical of the recent pattern: not only an attempt to create
order by asserting so-called traditional values but also an
attempt to keep away chaos by identifying an all-powerful
enemy responsible for chaos. For Meir Kahane, it is Ar-
abs; for the American religious right, it is secular humanism; for Ayatollah Ruhollah Khomeini, it was the United
States. For Farrakhan, it is Jews.

There is a very real and frightening despair to which
Farrakhan is speaking. It is the despair created when a nation persists in regarding blacks as a different species
rather than as individuals seeking to make the best of the
all-too-brief time each of us has on this earth. What are

blacks supposed to think when a mob of white teenagers in New York beats and hounds a black man until he runs onto an expressway and is killed? It does not inspire rousing choruses of "This Land Is My Land."

But such an incident is dramatic and the criminal-justice system caught the perpetrators and successfully prosecuted them. What happens to a significant number of blacks is not dramatic — which makes it, perhaps, all the more real.

The *New York Times* of January 26, 1987, reported that

> the nation's largest cities have a growing concentration of blacks living in poverty. While the overall rate of poverty in the nation increased slightly from 1970 to 13 percent in 1980, the number of people in poverty in the 50 cities jumped 11.7 percent at a time when the cities were losing population. The number of poor whites, however, declined 18 percent to 2,600,000, while the number of poor blacks rose 18 percent, to 3,140,000. In 1985 when unemployment among white adults was 5.6 percent, among black adults it was 14.9 percent. In 1984 one-half of black men aged 16 to 24 had no work experience at all.

It does not require great intelligence to understand that human beings, in pain and without hope, are behind those figures. What were whites trying to tell blacks at a time when white unemployment was declining and the stock market was setting record highs? There seems to be only one conclusion: white people don't care about black life. White people don't care if blacks live or die.

When one considers that one-half of black men between sixteen and twenty-four have no work experience, it is clear that white people must lack even a modicum of

intelligence. If that were not so, whites would quickly recognize the danger to themselves represented by a generation of black men without hope. This is a generation of
black men who have no reason to believe in democracy:
they certainly cannot believe that America is a land of opportunity and that adherence to the work ethic will pay
sumptuous dividends. White America will not even offer
them work, will not believe in their potential, will not care
if they die.

It is this despair and anger Louis Farrakhan exploits. I
say "exploits" because he certainly does not have a viable
program or an effective political organization to help alleviate the conditions. What Farrakhan does have is an
anti-Semitic message to which a significant number of
blacks respond.

When Louis Farrakhan appeared at Madison Square
Garden on October 7, 1985, it was apparent that he had
become America's preeminent black leader. Benjamin
Hooks of the NAACP could not have filled the Garden.
There would not have been people standing against the
walls to hear John Jacob of the National Urban League.
Jesse Jackson might have filled the Garden. But Farrakhan
filled not only the 20,000-plus seats; he also drew another
3,000 to 5,000 people to watch and listen on closed-cir-
cuit television in the Felt Forum next door.

If a people get the leader they deserve, then something
dire has happened in black America. No people should
make the journey from Martin Luther King, Jr., to Louis
Farrakhan in less than twenty years. These were not curious spectators or passive sympathizers. They were there to
applaud, cheer, yell, and shout. What they came to voice
approval of was apparent from the beginning.

One of the first speakers, whose job was to warm up
the audience for Farrakhan, was Kwame Toure, head of
the All-African People's Revolutionary party. When I

worked with him in SNCC in the late sixties, he was Stokely Carmichael. Seeing him on the stage at Madison Square Garden was like watching an "I Love Lucy" rerun. His face was the same; so were his words: "We are not poor; we are poorly organized!" "Our people don't need talk, they need guns!" These tepid leftovers from the sixties were cheered lustily, but the standing ovations were reserved for Toure's attacks on Israel, Zionism, and Judaism. "Africa gave Judaism to the world," he shouted to the great glee of the crowd. Citing Freud's *Moses and Monotheism* as evidence, he went on to claim: "Moses was an Egyptian! Moses was an African!"

A representative of the Palestinian Congress of America, Said Arafat, continued the history lesson: "Zionism is the cancer, and the supporters of Zionism are cancerous!" To the approval of the crowd, he concluded: "We want nothing but the total liberation of Palestine!" The next speaker was Russell Means of the American Indian Movement. A tall, muscular figure with two long, thin braids down his shirtfront, Means furthered what was to become the evening's litany when he talked about "those who controlled Hollywood. They have made movies denigrating and stereotyping Indians, Mexicans, Asians, and blacks. Never have you seen a movie denigrating the Jewish people!"

The audience greeted each anti-Semitic thrust by rising to its feet, cheering, arms outstretched at forty-five-degree angles, fists clenched. As this scene repeated itself throughout the evening, I wondered, Is this what it was like at the Nuremberg rallies in Nazi Germany?

Finally, flanked by six women in white hats and white suits with red tassels at the shoulders, Farrakhan walked onto the red-carpeted dais. More than 20,000 people rose, cheering and applauding, arms angled heavenward. Farrakhan stepped to the edge of the stage and stood motionless, arms outstretched from the waist as if he was posing as the Lamb of God. I didn't know it then, but he was.

The main item on the evening's agenda was to proclaim that Farrakhan is the Voice of Holy Truth whom Jews are determined to silence. "Somebody has to come to separate God from Satan, slavemaster and slave, oppressor and oppressed, so they can see each other and then go to war to see who is going to rule — God or Satan," he declared.

This is politico-religious fundamentalism at its most fanatical. This is fundamentalism as the ideology of power, representing itself as the only salvation from a primeval chaos that is sitting on the doorstep. This is fundamentalism that sees political and social reality as Armageddon and all those who are attempting to defeat the evil of primeval chaos as righteous crusaders and saviors.

At the head of the righteous is, of course, Farrakhan himself. He accused those who call him "Hitler-like" of seeking to "create an environment of hostility" in which someone might feel justified in assassinating him. But when Farrakhan anoints himself the representative of Truth and Salvation, comparisons to Hitler must follow.

"Who are those who support me? The righteous! You have been deprived of justice, and if God sends a deliverer, will the oppressor love him?" he asked the audience.

"*No!*" the crowd thundered.

"Are the Jews who are angry with me righteous people?"

"*No!*"

Farrakhan left no doubt that he is the Messiah: "Jesus had a controversy with the Jews. Farrakhan has a controversy with the Jews. Jesus was hated by the Jews. Farrakhan is hated by the Jews. Jesus was scourged by Jews in their temple. Farrakhan is scourged by Jews in their synagogues. Did Jesus care for the oppressed?"

"*Yes!*"

"They called him a devil. They call me a devil. When Jesus raised Lazarus from the dead and fed the five thousand [the miracle of the loaves and fishes], it was then that the authorities began to attack him. I am resurrecting the minds of black people from the dead, and they attack Farrakhan."

Farrakhan considers himself the only force capable of saving America. "What do you think will happen to America if anything happens to me? I am your last chance. America, you killed your last black leader when you killed Martin Luther King, Jr.!" Again, the audience roared and rose to its feet, arms thrust out, fists clenched.

"I am your last chance, too, Jews!" The audience laughed loudly and long. "The scriptures charge your people with killing the prophets of God." Farrakhan contended that God had not made the Jewish people pay for such deeds; however, if something happens to him, then God will make the Jews pay for all the prophets killed from biblical times to the present. "You cannot say 'never again' to God, because when God puts you in the oven, 'never again' don't mean a thing. If you fool with me, you court death itself. I will not run from you; I will run to you."

As a Jew, I was frightened, not so much by Farrakhan's words as by the response to them. It is one thing to read the words of political, racial, and religious anti-Semitism in books; it is another to hear them spoken with intensity, urgency, and conviction, to hear them affirmed with cheers, stamping feet, laughter, applause, and arms thrust toward heaven.

As a black, I was ashamed. What was happening in black America that it would revel in vicarious bloodletting? I know of the despair, of the poverty, of what it is to live beneath the relentless heat of racism, but this generation of blacks is not the first to make its way through the valley of the shadow of death. This generaton is the first, however, to wear its suffering as if it were a tiara. This generation is the first to use its suffering as if suffering bestowed a divine right exempting it from moral and ethical responsibility to the rest of humanity. But perhaps that is because this generation is the first to be without hope.

It does not speak well for the moral health of the black community that the black politicians and intellectuals who know better have been silent too often.

It is not Farrakhan who must be opposed. It is those who give him a hearing. One man is merely that — a solitary agony searching for a moment of relief or salvation between the cradle and the coffin. But when the solitary agony becomes a collective agony, to speak only of the man is wrong. Not to speak of the people who give him credence and legitimacy partakes of evil.

When Farrakhan shouted, "Who were the enemies of Jesus?" and all too many blacks shouted back, "Jews! Jews! Jews!" I knew that evil was sitting astride the land like Death on a pale horse.

The time has come to stop making apologies for blacks, to stop patronizing blacks with that paternalistic brand of understanding which finds excuses for the obscenities of hatred and anti-Semitism on the part of blacks. The time has come to say to black America that no amount of agony, no amount of poverty, deprivation, or suffering, justifies hatred, anti-Semitism, or the elevation of Louis Farrakhan to the position of spokesman and leader.

Even more, however, the time has come to say that Jews are Farrakhan's scapegoat but all of America is his victim. Farrakhan's anti-Semitism is a threat to what little moral fabric America has left. The way he revels in anti-Semitism, coupled with the absence of forceful responses against it by other blacks, makes Jew-hatred acceptable to blacks, educated and uneducated.

It requires no effort to hate. Farrakhan's anti-Semitism is an appeal to the comfort and sloth of hatred. He is subtly but surely creating an atmosphere in America in which hatreds of all kinds will be easier to express openly; and one day, in some as-yet-unknown form, these hatreds will ride the commuter trains to the suburbs. By then, it will be too late for us all.

Elie Wiesel has said it many times: he who hates Jews hates humanity. That is what is most distressing about black America's acceptance of Farrakhan. Why can't blacks see that Farrakhan hates them, too?

Jesse Jackson

✧✧✧

It was an exercise in sixties nostalgia. "Our time has come!" he shouted from the pulpits of black churches and the campaign stump. "Our time has come!"

The cry was reminiscent of the "Freedom Now!" chant of the early civil-rights movement, which was one recast and sung by Jim Morrison and the Doors in the late sixties as "We want the world and we want it now!" Both those chants may or may not have been effective mass psychology, but neither had any relation to effective politics. Neither did "Our time has come!"

Jesse Jackson's race for power in 1984 (disguised as a presidential candidacy) was taken more seriously than it might have been because he was black. (One could call blackness "the inherent intimidation factor.") An unfortunate legacy of the sixties is the almost total moral abdication on the part of whites so far as anything black is concerned. Having been told that they are "racists" because they have white skin, that they cannot understand blacks regardless of how much they educate themselves about black history and culture, most whites take refuge (publicly, at least) by patronizing and pitying blacks — by accepting, excusing, and rationalizing actions, attitudes, and words they would not accept from nonblacks.

> Jackson is now making history [proclaimed the *New York Times*], not as a black Presidential candidate but as a "serious" black Presidential candidate. That development alone is likely to have far-reaching effects on the American political scene by energizing the black vote and by altering the perceptions among whites of black candidates for elective office. (Quoted in *Playboy,* June 1984)

Such enthusiastic paternalism made the Jackson candidacy almost unassailable. (The truth is that FDR and JFK "energized" the black vote like no other candidates in American history; and if "the perceptions among whites of black candidates" had not already changed before Jackson entered the race, there would not have been so many black mayors.) Paternalism was nowhere more evident than in how the media allowed Jackson to survive his "Hymie/Hymietown" gaffe and his association with Minister Farrakhan. Walter Mondale and Gary Hart would not have survived as candidates in 1984 had they made references to "nigger" or "niggertown," or had they associated with reactionary white extremists, if for no other reason than that blacks would have gone to war! Jackson and the black community, however, were patronized by white liberals and the media — told, in effect, "You do not have to conform to the same ethical standards required of everyone else in our society."

But in an age when the "show-biz factor" permeates American life and presidential candidates are judged as much on that as their programs, Jackson's blackness, sex appeal, and messianic oratory allowed him to walk around in public "with no clothes on," and not even a child pointed it out.

Since the assassination of Martin Luther King, Jr., Jackson has been running for the position of heir apparent, which he began to achieve with his 1979 trip to Israel and Lebanon. The trip — his being photographed embracing Yasir Arafat, his pro-PLO and anti-Semitic statements — made him anathema to Jews; but blacks saw one of their own — handsome, well-dressed, articulate — making pronouncements on foreign policy and meeting with world leaders. Suddenly, Jackson was more than a charismatic black minister who headed a quasipolitical organization. He had become a symbol.

One who assumes the role of Deliverer becomes the repository for the dreams and aspirations of his group. He articulates the anguish and carries the hope for salvation. The messianic element enters politics when a people's despair is so total that they can conceive of no alternative to hopelessness. The seventies and the eighties were not good for many blacks. Unemployment of depression proportions, loss of real income, and the Reagan budget cuts were a cruel follow-up to the hopes raised in the sixties. Combining an expressed concern for the poor and the dispossessed with a perceived international standing, Jackson became a symbol that reaching the Promised Land was still possible for those who had almost forgotten it existed.

When Jackson announced for the presidency, hopes and dreams were unleashed as they had not been since the sixties. That those dreams and hopes were only going to be toyed with was apparent when Jackson said he was going to create a "Rainbow Coalition." A romantic phrase with overtones of the sixties, it seemed to promise a political Woodstock, an eternal People's Park, a perpetual March on Washington. (It was also a phrase with cultural associations. Was Jackson announcing that he was the new Wizard of Oz, and was I the only who kept expecting Judy

Garland to appear at a Jackson rally singing "Over the Rainbow"?)

"Rainbow Coalition" also had racial overtones, despite Jackson's insistence that it was "not an ethnic march, [but] a political movement to pull together the strength of rejected groups . . . to serve more effectively and be served better by their Government" (ibid.).

Jackson's explanation ignored a fundamental lesson of American history: a coalition of "rejected groups" has never brought about social change. Only when "rejected groups" are joined in a coalition by liberals and radicals from established groups has change occurred. The civil-rights movement was successful in fighting segregation and acquiring voting rights for blacks (and many others) only as long as that movement was composed of blacks together with white liberals and radicals. When "the movement" went its black-separatist way, its political effectiveness came to an abrupt end. The very concept on which Jackson's candidacy was based limited its appeal, ensuring Jackson the black vote and little else.

From the concept came another point of confusion: Jackson never seemed clear as to who he was. As one member of the Congressional Black Caucus, who did not want to be identified, put it, "The problem with Jesse is that he doesn't know what he wants to be, a politician making compromises or a civil rights leader saying 'I demand justice'" (*New York Times,* July 20, 1984). Jackson seemed to want to be Martin Luther King and Adam Clayton Powell. He talked alternately in the specifics of politics — the budget, foreign policy, and so on — and in the language of a moral crusade. "The rainbow is a moral cause, not just a political campaign" (ibid., July 1, 1984).

Any claim Jackson may have had to moral leadership was severely damaged by his "Hymie/Hymietown" remark, and was destroyed by his initial denials and belated admission of guilt. In other words, he lied, thus showing himself to be not a moral leader but a run-of-the-mill politician who, when caught with his foot in his mouth, instinctively denies that it is, indeed, his foot. But anyone who had followed Jackson's career knew that he was a walking repository of anti-Jewish clichés.

Even when denying that he was anti-Semitic, he proved the contrary. Jackson claimed that the term "Hymie" did not have a "negative meaning to it, either politically or religiously. It was an unfortunate use of words, but no different from someone saying he's going up to Harlem to see 'Mose' or 'Mosela.'" Interestingly, Jackson got on his racial high horse when Bill Moyers, in an interview, referred to him as the "Kingfish of politics," and then had to dismount in embarrassment when Moyers explained that he was referring to the former governor of Louisiana, Huey Long, and not the character on the late "Amos 'n' Andy" show.

Jackson's claims to morally superior leadership lost any semblance of credibility by his association with Louis Farrakhan of the Nation of Islam.

Why did Jackson associate himself with Farrakhan and why was he reluctant to end that association? Politically, Jackson did not need Farrakhan. According to Thomas N. Todd, Jackson's successor at Operation Push and the man who brought Jackson and Farrakhan together, it was an opportunity to put an end to splits between black civil-rights leaders and black nationalists (*New York Times,* June 30, 1984).

Such specious reasoning has plagued black American history for more than a century. This "race philosophy" is based on the premise that blackness is the overriding principle on which to create black unity. It is a reactionary nationalism that appeals to the lowest common denominator.

Jackson changed masks as it seemed to suit him, and became a race leader, moral figure, and politician by turns. The result was that he awoke one morning with Farrakhan around his neck like a noose. There is no doubt that the moral giants of black history — Douglass, Du Bois, King — would not have been associated with a Farrakhan. Each took the risk in his political career of articulating positions that were contrary to the prevailing black ethos, and each took it because he placed ethical principles above race.

Jackson could not repudiate Farrakhan because it would appear that he had given in to the demands of Jews to dissociate himself from the Black Muslim leader. The psychology of the race philosophy dictates a rallying around the black flag whenever a prominent black is attacked by whites. Sadly, no one asks if that black might have done something to merit being attacked.

Jackson missed a precious opportunity to demonstrate his moral leadership when he failed to repudiate Farrakhan immediately and to stand forthrightly against black anti-Semitism. One suspects, however, that Jackson could not do any of this because, unconsciously, Farrakhan was saying what Jackson could not.

In his speech at the Democratic convention in 1984, Jackson tried to reestablish his moral credentials.

> If in my low moments, in word, deed, or attitude, through some error of temper, taste, or tone, I have caused anyone discomfort, created pain, or revived someone's fears, that was not my truest self. If there were occasions when my grape turned into a raisin and my joy bell lost its resonance, please forgive me. Charge it to my head and not to my heart.

From the thunderous applause and cheers that greeted these words, one would have thought that Jackson had apologized. But apologies do not begin with a qualifying "if." Could Jackson doubt that he had "caused discomfort, created pain," and "revived fears"? His "apology" had all the earmarks of sincerity without honesty (as someone observed of James Agee).

Despite the almost universal approval given Jackson's speech, he gave no indication that he appreciated the depth of his moral confusion about Judaism and anti-Semitism. In his June 1984 *Playboy* interview, Jackson said: ". . . from a religious standpoint, there is something about Judaism that appeals to me. I'm Judaeo-Christian; my religous roots are there." To a religious Jew, such a statement smacks of arrogance. Because Jackson has read what Christians call the Old Testament does not mean he knows anything about Judaism (though Christians often make the mistake of equating Judaism with their Old Testament). It smacks of religious anti-Semitism by making Judaism a hyphenated prefix to Christianity. (There is no such religion as "Judaeo-Christian.") Jackson maintained that "historically, the best experience of the Jewish people has been in their religious faith, the chastising, courageous strength of the prophets who challenged their own politicians." It is precisely this lecturing of others about their experience that blacks have objected to angrily when they have been on the receiving end.

Jackson's political acumen could be as questionable as his morality. While political radicals and some liberals may have found solace in his positions on Central America, the defense budget, and gay rights, for example, his radicalism put him to the left of the black electorate and the Democratic party. Jackson's trips to Nicaragua and Cuba and his statements in support of their governments did not endear him to the mainstream.

The measure of politicians is, ultimately, their effectiveness in meeting the needs of a constituency. Jackson could

never seem to decide whether his campaign was a serious
political effort on behalf of blacks and the economically
dispossessed or only a symbolic, ego-assuaging moment in
the klieg lights.

He may have succeeded on the symbolic level but, in a
curious way, his 1984 candidacy was out of step with both
the black mood and the national mood. A *New York
Times*/CBS News poll (July 10, 1984) revealed little difference in attitudes among blacks and whites on defense
spending, but reduction in defense spending was a major
Jackson issue. Another of his issues was the abolition of
runoff primaries in the South. Yet, the same poll revealed
that only 15 percent of Jackson's avowed supporters
agreed with him.

The thrust of Jackson's campaign was in defiance of what
had been quietly happening for the previous fifteen years.
Jackson ignored the fact that blacks had been getting
elected to major offices in cities where white support was
necessary, and they had been doing so without the fairy-
tale imagery of rainbows. Coleman Young in Detroit, Wil-
son Goode in Philadelphia, Tom Bradley in Los Angeles,
Harold Washington in Chicago, and Thirman Milner in
Hartford could not have been elected with black votes
only. And Bradley came within 1 percent of being elected
governor of California — a feat that clearly needed white
votes.

Jackson's plaint throughout the 1984 campaign that
whites were not as liberal as blacks because blacks would
vote for whites but whites would not vote for blacks is
simply not true. His comment was an insult to the black
politicians who have presented themselves to the voters of
their communities on their merits as politicians and administrators, and not as symbols of a cause.

Jackson's attempt to meld a moral appeal with politics
failed because the days when blacks can make moral

claims on the white conscience are over. Such claims have not only lost their effectiveness, they have acquired an air of black self-pity.

But Jackson is a product of the sixties, and the style of his candidacy in 1984 was covered with the dust of civil-rights marches. However, the substance that made the civil-rights movement successful was lacking — a wedding of tactics to meet the problem, an involvement of blacks and whites in action to create change, an idealism that sought not utopia but respect for the integrity of all human beings. The civil-rights movement awakened hope and gave it purpose and focus.

With one hand, Jackson seemed to offer through his Rainbow Coalition a renewal of the black-Jewish-liberal coalition of the civil-rights movement. With the other, he seemed concerned only with creating a black constituency. Ultimately, there is something immoral about a campaign slogan that says, "Our time has come!" because an "our" automatically creates a "their" whose time must end.

Despite the "Rainbow" rhetoric, there was a tone of meanness in such a slogan — meanness because it was a rhetoric that excluded. But that is in the nature of a cause. Causes are waged on behalf of a particular group and are aimed against those who do not belong to the group.

I had hoped that with the assassination of Martin Luther King, Jr., blacks would cease investing their dreams and hopes in a leader, that they would eschew causes and instead begin to take responsibility as a group for the problems faced by the group, regardless of who created the problems.

Instead, the Rainbow Coalition of 1984 gave way to the politics of the messiah in 1988. Many seem to have no trouble recognizing the messiahs of the political and religious right, but remain blind to the fact that messiahs can also come from the left. When a white factory worker in Wisconsin was quoted in the press as saying that he voted for George Wallace in 1968 and would vote for Jesse Jackson in 1988, it should have been obvious that political ideologies are secondary to the need for salvation.

Jackson is widely applauded for his ability to articulate the despair and hopes of blacks, the poor, the dispossessed, and so on. But the answer Jackson offers is not community organizing, protest, or anything remotely related to a social movement in which the people affected would be the instruments for the needed change.

This is where Jackson differs from the man whose heir he claims to be. Martin Luther King, Jr., never offered himself as the means for the solution to segregation and voter disenfranchisement.

What was most distressing about Jackson's 1988 campaign was that a significant sector of the population, black and white, fell under a mass delusion. When a people, any people, invests its hopes and dreams in a leader and does so with the energy and almost mass hysteria that surrounded the Jackson campaign, the result can only be bitter disappointment, because no individual can be a savior.

And yet, there is something deep within the human psyche that wants to believe in saviors, that is ready to listen and respond to anyone who says he will solve our problems. Thus, Jackson and black America are like Siamese twins joined together at the hip who gaze into each other's face and see not the other but themselves.

Unfortunately, Jackson's political career will not be as short-lived as a rainbow. Nor will it fill our spirits with a sense of wonder and awe, making us feel we can be more than we are.

The Responsibility of the Black Intellectual

✧✧✧

In February of 1988, I lectured at a West Coast university on relations between Jews and blacks. I had given the lecture at many schools, for a number of years, and have respected the blacks in attendance as they struggled to come to terms with me, a black and a Jew — a combination that must have made me seem like a sociological mutant.

But that February night, for the first time, there was hostility in the postlecture questions, hostility that increased and intensified with each question from a black student. Eventually, blacks and Jews in the audience were yelling at each other, and the rhetorical violence threatened to become physical. To prevent that, I left the stage and the confrontation ended. Later that month, at a small private college in the East, I encountered a similar hostility from black students.

In mid-March 1988, the Department of Afro-American Studies at the University of Massachusetts at Amherst formally asked the administration to "reassign" me to another department. The ostensible reason was what the

180

department characterized as my "deliberate misrepresentations" of the novelist James Baldwin in my then just-published book *Lovesong: Becoming a Jew.*

The actual reasons were perhaps more directly expressed when Professor Chester Davis, then department chairman, was quoted in the *Amherst Bulletin* as saying, "We have nothing against his Judaism . . . but when one develops a vicious attitude toward blacks and black organizations, Jackson, Baldwin and civil rights, there is some question as to the appropriateness of his remaining in the department."

The dean of the Faculty of Humanities and Fine Arts, Murray Schwartz, told me that Professor Davis had said to him, "If you don't get Lester out of the department, we'll make his life miserable." In a public statement endorsed by all fifteen members of the department, I was characterized as "the anti-Negro Negro" who sought "compulsively to slay the birth-people enemy who exist in his malicious and unforgiving imagination."

It is possible that such statements revealed nothing more than a succumbing to the temptation of hyperbole. But when I met hostility from black students at opposite ends of the country, when blacks on radio call-in shows in New York City, Detroit, and Boston told me that the department was right to ask for my reassignment, that I should "make aliya" (emigrate) to Israel as soon as possible, and that, having become a Jew, I could no longer be considered black, I reluctantly concluded that the Department of Afro-American Studies was merely reflecting the intellectual climate in black America.

Twenty-five years ago, the Reverend Dr. Martin Luther King, Jr., Malcolm X, Adam Clayton Powell, Jr., Roy Wilkins, Whitney Young, James Farmer, and the Student Nonviolent Coordinating Committee, among others, argued and publicly debated the philosophies, tactics, and strategies of the civil-rights movement. The arguments were sometimes bitter, but the fact of disagreement was accepted as normal.

Such debate and diversity of opinion are absent today. When a student at the School of the Art Institute of Chicago exhibited a painting satirizing the late mayor Harold Washington, the school removed the painting after an angry reaction from blacks. Yet, neither the Reverend Jesse Jackson nor any other black leader objected.

Are black self-esteem and self-confidence so insecure that a student's painting threatens the black self-image? Is black identity so problematic that one is to be judged an "anti-Negro Negro" for being critical of James Baldwin and Jesse Jackson? Despite all the rhetoric of black pride in the past twenty-five years, is pride an insufficient attribute for the creation of a cohesive and mature group identity?

It is not easy to write such words in an intellectual climate that confuses criticism with assault. But the responsibility of the intellectual, black or white, male or female, is to stand outside in order to better describe what is occurring inside. In black America today, intellectuals are too often silent. What is missing is a moral sensitivity and sensibility.

In 1984, black academics and intellectuals were silent when Jackson referred to Jews as "Hymies." They were silent in the face of anti-Semitic remarks by Louis Farrakhan. In 1988, they were silent when Steve Coakley, an aide to then Mayor Eugene Sawyer of Chicago, said that Jews were responsible for the AIDS virus. They were silent when the satiric painting of Harold Washington was removed from the walls of the exhibition.

I know that black intellectuals are not morally insensitive, but there comes a time when silence becomes immoral complicity, when the exaltation of blackness over democratic values becomes a political fundamentalism no different from the religious fundamentalism that threatens white America. The goal of each is to remake the nation in its particular image. But the democratic ideal is a nation composed of many images, especially those I may not like.

While many would prefer to dismiss my experience with the Department of Afro-American Studies as a problem of personalities, it is not. Justice Felix Frankfurter wrote that teachers "are the priests of our democracy" because their task is "to foster those habits of open-mindedness and critical inquiry which alone make for responsible citizens." Teachers work, he wrote, by "precept and practice, by the very atmosphere which they generate; they must be exemplars of open-mindedness and free inquiry."

The threat to open-mindedness and free inquiry being posed by many black intellectuals and the increasing presence of a spirit that equates critical inquiry with malevolent opposition are not only a threat to the souls of black folks, they are a threat to America itself.

Falling Pieces
of the
Broken
Sky

Objects

✧✧✧

When my father died, one of the tasks that fell to me was to sort through the minutiae of his life and decide which objects to save and which to throw away.

Now I look at the objects of my life as if I were dead, wondering, what will my children do with the human skull that sits on the bookcase next to my desk? I couldn't blame them if they threw it out. They've been wanting to do that for some years, but will they know how much can be learned from living with a skull? And what about my books? Surely they can find someplace in their apartments for ten thousand books. However, I know they will look at the white, plastic head of a horse on my desk and throw it into a Glad trash bag without a thought, never knowing that it is the only piece remaining from the first chess set I owned. It is me at age twelve.

But that is the order of things. The final decisions about who we were are left to those who knew us least — our children. I was the closest to my father and knew him well, and yet, only when I was going through his study did I learn he had collected picture postcards of hotels. Had he

187

ever shown the huge scrapbook to anyone? And what was I to do with it now?

What was I to do with all the objects that had been him? The grieving part of me wanted to put everything in my car and take it home. The rational prevailed, however, and I filled trash bag after trash bag with old newspapers, magazines, paper clips, pamphlets of all kinds, apologizing to his spirit as I did. I could not throw out the thousands of slides he had taken on his travels. He was not an artistic photographer; he was not a good one even, but he was a loving one. I brought the slides home, though I will never look at them. And I brought home the postcards, too. I brought twelve boxes of my father home.

How many boxes of me will my children keep? Or will they look in the yellow pages under Trash Hauling and tell some unshaven man with a cigar in his jaw to take me to the landfill?

Can I trust my children with my life? How would they know that the tiny replica of a samovar sitting on a windowsill of my study is a miniature of the one Tolstoy used? Every object of our lives is a memory, and emotion swirls around it like fog, hiding and protecting a tiny truth of the heart.

I look at the objects that are my life and the only way my children can satisfy me is by not touching a thing. But they must if they are to go on with their lives. They must if I am to go on with my death.

I look at these objects that are me and know, too, that they are symbols of how alone I am, how alone each of us is, for no one knows what any object means except he or she who owns it. Only I have the memories of when and how each one was acquired; only I have the memory of taking it home like one of my newly born children from the hospital; only I have the memory of what it looked like when I lived in that apartment and where it sat in that house.

I look at the objects that are me and the memories are warm and permeated with love. I look at the objects that are me and know that I'm going to miss me very much.

Windchill

✧ ✧ ✧

What is the windchill factor?

I know it is some arcane formula whereby the temperature and wind velocity are calculated together and the result is how cold it *feels* as opposed to what the air temperature is. Obviously, whoever thought of the windchill factor did not have four children. Those of us who do spend our days calculating the stress factor.

The salient question is, does humanity need the windchill factor? Do we really need to know at seven in the morning (or any other time of day) that it feels like sixty below zero outside?

No.

For most of the thousands and thousands of years there have been people on earth, there was no windchill factor. Indeed, most people in the world today not only do not know the windchill factor, they don't even know the temperature. It is sufficient to know that it is cold, and that when the wind is blowing, it is *really* cold.

Isn't that all we need to know? When I hear on the weather report that it feels like sixty below, I am receiving information for which I have no use. It certainly does not make me eager to leave the house. It is not the Rosetta stone that will unlock the secret to surviving my children's adolescence. And the bank will not accept the windchill factor as a reason for skipping this month's mortgage. The windchill factor is about as useless a piece of information to be inflicted on the American people since *Time* published photographs of Tricia Nixon's wedding.

Why, then, has the windchill factor become so important? Perhaps it has something to do with another kind of chill that has settled on the land, a chill whose source cannot be located and whose effects we do not know how to counter. That is the chill we experience in an economy that becomes increasingly incomprehensible and unsure. It is the chill engendered by living in a world in which the threat of nuclear annihilation is omnipresent, a world whose fate is in the hands of people whose IQs have a number about the same as the windchill factor.

Helpless to alleviate the chill, we seize on a chill that can be measured. Though we can't alleviate it, it is clear that we are being asked to endure and by enduring a winter of windchill factors of thirty, forty, fifty below zero, we emerge into spring with a pathetic sense of heroism.

But once, people lived on this land and endured winters without knowing the temperature, not to mention the windchill factor, and also without central heating, down-filled parkas, triple-insulated windows, or latex caulking for their tent flaps.

There is no heroism to be found in surviving winter, regardless of the windchill factor. Heroes and heroines are those who find the ways to triumph over that chill which causes the human spirit to shiver and fear for its survival.

Voyager

✧ ✧ ✧

I looked at the photographs *Voyager I* was sending back of the rings of Saturn and chuckled as the rings around the planet seemed to increase with each day — fifty, a hundred, five hundred, a thousand. Some rings were braided like loaves of challah, while other rings were lopsided, and in some, spokes formed. The rings of Saturn defied all theories about rings. "The bizarre has become the commonplace," said one scientist, and I breathed a sigh of relief.

Voyager sent back images of the previously unseen, and we saw and did not know what we saw. "Those spokes are giving us nightmares," commented one astronomer. How comforting.

Once, an African student told me a story about how, when he was a child, he would go out from his village at night to count the stars. He counted for many nights, often losing his place and having to start over, but he persisted until one night his father asked what he was doing.

"I'm counting the stars."

"You mustn't do that," his father admonished him. "There are some things only God is supposed to know."

Such respect for the natural world is an attitude foreign

to the Western sensibility. We climb mountains because they are there. Carl Sagan contends that we must explore space because "the exploratory instinct is deeply built into us and possibly an important part of the success of ourselves as a species."

How Western and how male.

What "success" have we as a species achieved? We have not learned to live with ourselves and one another. What Sagan defines as the "exploratory instinct" may be nothing more than "flight response," the compulsion to flee the dilemma of being human, to escape the terror-filled encounter with ourselves that is the only means by which we can be human.

Western man has never gone forth to explore. That is the heroic rationalization for the need to conquer. Nothing remains to be vanquished now except space, and it must be conquered — for, as Spengler wrote, space is terrifying because of its "cognate sense of annihilation." How alone and how insignificant we are in the face of an infinite universe, the ultimate unknowable.

Perhaps that is what *Voyager* sent back its photographs to tell us. There is a limit to what we are to know, and the way through the human dilemma is in the wonder and mystery of lopsided rings and spokes that should not be — and are.

Voyager attained the numinosity of a god for me because it gave the opportunity to know anew that awe which is more indispensable to our species than any so-called exploratory instinct.

It was autumn of 1980 when god-*Voyager* sent back its photographs of Saturn's rings. The day it left our solar system, there was a number one could call to hear *Voyager's* signal as it crossed into outer space. I called and listened to a steady beeping and was enthralled.

Voyager will wander for a billion years as an emissary from Earth, carrying a phonograph record with samples of the music of this planet: Bach, of course, Chuck Berry, gamelan music, and more.

That record represents our reaching out to communicate with extraterrestrial life, which many are convinced must exist. I wonder.

I imagine god-*Voyager* in the silence of space, and even the Bach Brandenburg no. 2 must sound like noise in the depth of infinity's silence. For a billion years, god-*Voyager* will journey, carrying an offering of music from Earth.

What if, in all the universe, there is no one to listen?

What if, in all the universe, the conditions for life are possible on only one small planet in a tiny solar system at the edge of the Milky Way galaxy? What if we are alone in the universe?

Perhaps it is the terror of this aloneness that compels us to conquer space — first by accruing facts, and later through colonization. But we have not learned to live on this planet. What makes us think we could live any better in space?

Perhaps it is the terror of our aloneness in the universe that convinces others that there is life out there. We seem to need to believe in life on other worlds. We have projected our need for a messiah into outer space, hoping that something or someone will come and we shall yet be saved.

What would happen if we faced the terror and lived as if we are the only representatives of life in all the universe? All else is weird worlds of gases, seas of liquid nitrogen, or bleak landscapes of ice where winds blow for eternity at nine hundred miles per hour.

If we are the sole representatives of life, do we not have a sacred responsibility to life?

We will not be saved by any messianic close encounters of the third kind. We are all there is, all there has been, and all there will be — ever. If we are kind to ourselves, we will look at those photographs of Saturn, its rings and moons, and the mystery of what it is to be human will deepen within us.

It is a terror that partakes of the miraculous.

Teenage Suicides

✧✧✧

We are cruel to the young in America.

We have created a culture in which youth is an idol we bow to while offering our souls. We dye our hair, style it, and blow-dry it into illusory memories of what we looked like once. Each birthday after forty crashes down on us like a mountain, and we become ashamed. We fear that with the passing of youth, life passes. So we exercise and diet and apply lotions and creams and curse the wrinkles and layers of fat, which persist in being the truths that they are.

Because we worship youth, we unconsciously transform the young into idols. In television commercials, the middle-aged sell life insurance, denture cleaners, and laxatives. The young sell glamour and excitement — sleek automobiles, clothes, and frozen entrées we are to believe can rival the cooking of gourmet chefs.

Our idolization of youth is evident in how we treat adolescent athletes. We thrust microphones before a nineteen-year-old who has scored thirty-five points in a basketball game as if we expect him to be able to speak in something other than clichés. A teenage gymnast wins

196

Olympic gold medals and we make her into a national heroine.

And then, we pretend that we do not understand when the suicide rate among teenagers continues to rise. We are shocked and dismayed. Why would the young kill themselves?

We do not care to remember what it is like to be young. We do not want to remember that there is no glamour in youth. It is a time of uncertainty and fear. It is a time when you are no longer a child but neither are you an adult who has made a place in the world. Youth is a time of almost total self-doubt because you do not have a self that can stand amidst the world's confusions and complexities. Youth is a time of seeking for and needing self-definition without the skills or knowledge to achieve it.

By idolizing the young, we evade taking responsibility for them. We do not give them the care and protection and definitions they need to make that frightening transition from childhood to adulthood. But we do not take responsibility for being adults. And part of the responsibility of adulthood is taking responsibility for the young. We cannot do that as long as youth is the idolatrous temple in which we worship.

We are cruel to the young in America; and the young, unable to understand our cruelty, kill themselves; and we look into mirrors each morning and do not see ourselves.

We are cruel to the young in America.

Morality and Education

✧✧✧

The election of Ronald Reagan in 1980 brought to the center of national life a conflict that began with the 1954 *Brown v. Board of Education of Topeka* Supreme Court decision. The conflict is not expressed in the language of white against black, however, but in the rhetoric of religion. The enemy is not a race but a way of thinking called "secular humanism." The battlefield is the public schools.

Numerous parent groups demand "a return to many of the teaching practices and textbooks of 30 years ago, as well as the Christian values and principles upon which, they argue, the country was founded" (*New York Times*, May 17, 1981). Such groups are succeeding in efforts to ban "objectionable" books from schools, to eliminate sex education, new math, and creative-writing courses, and to teach the biblical story of creation in science classes. The battle is over "the very nature of public education itself," and what is to be decided, we are told, is whether America is a nation that believes in "the supremacy of man rather than the supremacy of God" (ibid., February 10, 1981).

It is too simple to maintain, as some do, that "secular humanism is a straw man. They are looking for someone to blame" (Paul Kirtz, quoted ibid., May 17, 1981). Nor is it particularly illuminating to define the attacks on secular humanism as a new McCarthyism that is substituting humanists for Communists. It is not so simple, because the underlying issue, first raised unintentionally by the *Brown* decision, is the all-important one of collective identity — that is: What does it mean to be an American?

The Supreme Court thought it knew that spring of 1954 when it decreed that the "equal protection of the law" enjoyed by the children of the white majority must be extended to the children of the black minority. An answer in the affirmative seems obvious, but in 1954 the white majority did not find it so. Didn't the black minority enjoy equal protection in its "separate but equal" schools? The Court had to convince the white majority what blacks had known since 1896: No.

The court posed for itself a simple question (or so it seemed): Were two schools, one white, one black — comparable in physical facilities and quality of teaching — unequal? The Court argued that there was not sufficient grounds for judgment.

> Our decision . . . cannot turn on merely a comparison of these tangible factors in the negro and white schools involved. . . . We must look instead to the effect of segregation itself on public education.
>
> We must consider public education in the light of its full development and its present place in American life through the nation. Only in this way can it be determined if segregation in public schools deprives these plaintiffs of the equal protection of the laws.

To do this, the Court found it necessary to define the role and function of education.

Today, education is perhaps the most important function of state and local governments. Compulsory school attendance laws and the great expenditures for education both demonstrate our recognition of the importance of education to our democratic society. It is required in the performance of our most basic public responsibilities, even service in the armed forces. It is the very foundation of good citizenship. Today it is a principal instrument in awakening the child to cultural values, in preparing him to adjust normally to his environment. In these days, it is doubtful that any child may reasonably be expected to succeed in life if he is denied the opportunity of an education. Such an opportunity, where the state has undertaken to provide it, is a right which must be made available to all on equal terms.

We come then to the question presented: Does segregation of children in public schools solely on the basis of race, even though the physical facilities and other "tangible factors may be equal, deprive the children of the minority group of equal education opportunities?" We believe that it does.

There was nothing revolutionary or startling in the Court's definition of education. It merely reiterated what already existed and used a philosophical context to demonstrate that the inclusion of black children was crucial. Why, then, was there such massive white resistance to the decision, a resistance and antagonism that would extend from the steps of Central High in Little Rock to the streets of South Boston two decades later?

In its decision, the Court decreed a major change in the nation's moral values without recognizing that it was doing so. The Court ended segregation in the schools, but without destroying the underlying moral value of white supremacy — a value it was oblivious of and a value it unintentionally upheld.

The revolutionary decision was based on the wrong premise — that "the children of the minority group" were deprived "of equal education opportunities." By making black "inferiority" the focus, the Court reinforced white "superiority."

> To segregate them [black children] from others of similar age and qualifications solely because of their race generates a feeling of inferiority as to their status in the community that may affect their hearts and minds in a way unlikely ever to be undone.

This statement of paternalistic concern and melodramatic excess confers the status and identity of generous benefactor on the white majority. Instead of attacking white supremacy, the Court confirms it.

> Segregation of white and colored children in public schools has a detrimental effect upon the colored children. The impact is greater when it has the sanction of the law; for the policy of separating the races is usually interpreted as denoting the inferiority of the negro group. A sense of inferiority affects the motivation of the child to learn. Segregation with the sanction of the law, therefore, has a tendency to [retard] the educational and mental development of negro children and to deprive them of some of the benefits they would receive in a racial[ly] integrated school system.

How different the course of recent American race relations and history would be if the above passage had read thus:

To segregate white children from others of similiar age and qualifications solely because of their race generates a feeling of superiority as to their status in the community that may affect their hearts and minds in a way unlikely ever to be undone.

Segregation of white and colored children in public schools has a detrimental effect upon the white children. The impact is greater when it has the sanction of the law; for the policy of separating the races is usually interpreted as denoting the superiority of the white group. A sense of superiority affects the motivation of the child to learn. Segregation with the sanction of law, therefore, has a tendency to [retard] the educational and mental development of white children and to deprive them of some of the benefits they would receive in a racial[ly] integrated school system.

The Court's decision did not provide a new context in which the white majority could have made sense of the revolutionary decree. Segregation had been accepted as a legal and moral truth since *Plessy v. Ferguson* in 1896. *Brown* established a new legal truth, but the moral truth extant since America's inception remained.

The white majority was placed in a quandary. Either they discovered for themselves a new moral truth by which to accept the revolution, or they resisted and refused to obey the "law of the land." Realistically, there was no course but the latter.

White resistance to school desegregation received official sanction on March 12, 1956, when 101 members of Congress issued a "Declaration of Constitutional Principles," reasserting segregation on legal and moral grounds.

The Supreme Court . . . unanimously declared, in 1927 . . . that the "separate-but-equal" principle is, "within the discretion of the state in regulating its public schools and does not conflict with the Fourteenth Amendment."

This interpretation, restated time and again, became a part of the life of the people of many of the states and confirmed their habits, customs, traditions, and way of life. It is founded on elemental humanity and common sense, for *parents should not be deprived by government of the right to direct the lives and education of their own children* [emphasis added].

Suddenly, the issue was not solely desegregation. A new one was introduced, which was inadequately characterized as states' rights versus federalism. The issue was more profound and involved a fundamental question of democracy: What was the legal and moral power of the people "to direct the lives and education of their own children"?

Brown represented the white majority's first experience with the power of government functioning in a manner inimical to that majority's perceived best interests. The Warren Court had done the inconceivable: it had spoken as advocate for the black minority and not on behalf of the white majority.

If the Court had been prescient enough to speak about the effects of white supremacy on whites as well as blacks, then it would have spoken for all the people. By speaking on behalf of the black minority, the Court threatened the white majority, not only in terms of the majority's identity but in its perceived right of self-determination.

White supremacy was, to use Frances FitzGerald's phrase, a "public truth," one the white majority was not prepared to relinquish. When whites bombed desegregated schools, when mobs gathered outside schools to curse and spit on black children, when the governor of Arkansas closed Central High in Little Rock to keep out nine black children, when southern congressmen commended "the motives of those states which have declared the intention to resist forced integration by any lawful means," they were not only expressing the moral power of white supremacy, they were expressing their resistance to an attack on their identities as Americans and their power to define their lives.

The white majority resisted the Court decree — by violence, legal maneuvering, and the establishment of private schools. (In the sixties and seventies, when school desegregation became an issue in the North and busing was implemented, white resistance took the forms of the "white flight to the suburbs," and finally, in 1981, a congressional prohibition against Justice Department involvement in busing as a solution to alleviate de facto segregation.) Instead of affirming the supremacy of the law, the white majority asserted that it would obey a morality higher than the law.

It is not usual to think of white supremacy as moral. However, it has been considered so by most of the white majority throughout American history. Morality defines and enforces collective standards of good and evil as well as what constitutes acceptable collective behavior. Morality can be subjective or objective, but for a society to be stable, subjective morality must correspond to objective morality. When the two deviate significantly, as happened in the sixties, the national identity is threatened. When a group of conservatives designates itself as a "Moral Majority," it is saying, in effect, that its subjective morality is no longer sufficiently reflected in the objective world. Significantly, the root of the word *moral* is "me, myself."

If one can recognize that "moral" does not necessarily mean good but only what a majority has agreed upon as good, then it is evident that white supremacy is moral; and until *Brown,* the morality of the white majority had been reflected by the federal government.

White supremacy is an integral part of America's structure and essential to American identity. *Brown* attacked that structure and identity. The white majority retaliated by disobeying the "law of the land" and reasserting the only morality it had.

White resistance to *Brown* had an effect no one could have foreseen: it helped create the civil-rights movement. The black minority was stunned by the white refusal to obey the Supreme Court and institute desegregation of schools with "all deliberate speed." If the white majority would break a law it considered unjust, then the black minority was free to break those laws it considered unjust. Civil disobedience and the breakdown in "law and order" decried by conservatives and placed at the doorsteps of blacks was the legacy of the same conservatives who fulminated against its breakdown.

However, there was a difference in the two kinds of lawbreaking. One sought to abrogate the law; the other sought to uphold democracy and its promise of equality before the law. One reaffirmed the national identity as it had always been; the other sought to create a new national identity. (It is impossible for blacks and other racial and religious minorities to have a cohesive national identity as long as white supremacy is a component of that identity.) One resisted the power of the federal government to dictate to local communities; the other had no alternative but to pressure the federal government to intervene more. Thus, the national identity became divided into conflicting moralities.

For a brief period, the morality of the black minority prevailed, with the indispensable support of a significant segment of the white majority. The desegregation of

America and the inclusion of blacks in the national identity that began with *Brown* continued with the 1964 Civil Rights Act and the 1965 Voting Rights Act. The conflicting moralities were not reconciled, however.

Indeed, the gulf between them intensified and widened, because a new generation of youths from the white majority found itself facing conscription to fight a war in Vietnam, a war for which the rationales of patriotism and the communist menace were not convincing. The refusal to obey the law of the land that began with white resistance to *Brown* and found new form in the civil-rights movement now acquired a life in a wholly different area — draft and war resistance.

Objective morality (patriotism, obedience to the state) was supplanted in the sixties by a subjective morality of personal responsibility and personal expression. "I'm doing my thing" was a moral call to arms, and new forms of cultural expression proliferated like dandelions on a poorly seeded lawn. From the midsixties through the seventies, subjective moralities gave the illusion of becoming the national identity in the usage of mind-altering drugs, sexual freedom, the human-potential movement, crafts cooperatives, women's liberation, gay liberation, abortion rights, and educational reforms.

Traditional morality had not disappeared, however. For almost a decade it was submerged, but it has resurfaced in many guises — the antiabortion movement, legal challenges to affirmative action — and, not to be overlooked, in the arena where the battle began in 1954: the schools.

The subjective morality that dominated the sixties had a great impact on education. Textbooks were rewritten to show that America was not all white and not always right. The new math replaced traditional arithmetic. The very process of learning was reconceptualized to reflect the subjective morality whose slogan was best expressed on a bumper sticker: "Question Authority." The classroom was reorganized and the teacher was no longer the authority but just another participant in "open classrooms" where all opinions were equal. And the school day no longer began with prayer.

Objective moralists had lost control of their schools when they were ordered to desegregate them. The educational reforms of the sixties and seventies took ideological control away from them. The schools had become a colosseum in which objective and subjective moralists were pitted against one another, each with their own version of the universe.

Where the objective moralist believed in patriotism, Christianity of the fundamentalist-Protestant variety, and children as Lockean blank slates, the new moralist emphasized the child as individual, personal relationships characterized by intimacy and gentleness, and the world as village. Neither recognized how much at home they both were in an America growing from Puritan roots, for both believed that morality should be the basis of education. Both yearned for theocracy, but only one admitted it. Cotton Mather is Billy Graham is "I'm O.K., You're O.K.," because a rose is a rose is a rose. The issue was, which side would be forced to wear a scarlet letter? Who would prevail when each had right on its side?

Where objective morality relies on Christianity to determine good and evil, subjective morality seeks sanction from a new religion: psychology. This is evident in the teacher's edition of the Houghton Mifflin social-studies series that claims to teach "strategies designed to increase empathy and decrease inclinations toward egocentrism, and stereotyping," while helping children make "valid judgments about problems facing our global society." (It is assumed that these are valid goals for children who are still trying to establish egos and group identities, and who may need stereotypes, for a while, to secure their own places in a world that is overwhelming. "Empathy" is assumed as a socialization value, without considering that empathy can lead to stasis. As in objective morality, the child is treated as an object. A change in ideology does not necessarily make for a change in substance.)

In its use of psychology, subjective morality in education is insidious, because it seeks social change. It wants to create persons. But as Frances FitzGerald observed in *America Revised*, "Until the twentieth century, few American educators believed that textbooks — or schooling in general — could or should be an instrument for changing the culture."

Brown targeted the schools as agents for social change. Children were asked to do what adults had shown little desire to do — create an integrated nation.

Subjective morality wants to use the schools to create "decent" human beings, and despite the differences in style, philosophy, and rhetoric, this is also the goal of objective morality. For one, the way is secular humanism. For the other, the way is Christian beliefs. Both moralities are asking the schools to assume the responsibility of parents. In the process, both are doing what each would vigorously deny: they are increasing the power of the state and making it Big Parent. Each is demanding that the state reflect its image and its image only. Each finds its moral version of the universe inadequate without state sanction.

The national identity is no longer in sharp relief. Unsure about the present and frightened by prospects for the future, Americans are asking the schools to embody that identity no longer extant in their lives or the society. They want the schools to do what should be done by the family, church, synagogue, or mosque.

The national identity has fragmented to such an extent since *Brown* that the white majority cannot face with equanimity that it is only one element in a democratic society. It insists that it must be the sole element, the moral majority.

With Reagan's election, the objective moralists achieved political power and sought to have their moral grievances redressed through the law. The attacks on abortion laws intensified, while laws requiring the teaching of the biblical creation story, laws restricting the employment opportunities of homosexuals, and the banning of books from schools and public libraries sought to institutionalize Christian morality.

The central question in the last decade of the twentieth century may be: Is the purpose of law the codification of morality? Or, does a redefinition of the national identity require a clear distinction in law between citizen and person? In her book *On Revolution,* Hannah Arendt wrote:

> A Roman citizen . . . had a *persona,* a legal personality. . . . The law had affixed to him the part he was expected to play on the public scene, with the provision, however, that his own voice would be able to sound through. The point was that "it is the natural Ego which enters a court of law. It is a right-and-duty-bearing person, created by the law, which appears before the law."

Neither the traditional nor the subjective moralists differentiate themselves as persons from themselves as citizens. Without such differentiation, law and morality become synonymous.

Thus, when the objective moralist cannot use the law,

group pressure is exerted to achieve the desired moral end. "We have to get rid of secular humanism," a superintendent of schools in South Dakota was quoted as saying, and that can be achieved by getting rid of "liberal, real liberal, personnel" (*New York Times,* May 17, 1981). Or books: in 1980, the American Library Association received between three and five reports a day of attempts to ban books from public-school libraries.

Public education has become the object of a holy war. The educational process itself has had a sacred aura conferred upon it. Such an aura is misplaced, because education cannot create the ideal society or restore the national identity. As the Warren Court made clear, education is a limited tool, a function of the state. Education is political; its aim is the creation of citizens.

Morality belongs to the sphere of religion or the individual. It confers group and/or individual identity. When morality is used to confer national identity, the fabric of democracy is threatened; democracy's vitality and strength lies in a diversity of belief, opinion, and practice contained within a legal framework that protects the citizen from the state and from the morality of the majority.

Education must be separated from morality, objective and subjective, and narrowed to its most basic function — the transmission of the political values the state finds necessary for its continuation. It is naive to expect any state, democratic or totalitarian, to do other than require public education to transmit a glorified image of the nation: its history, culture, the fundamental principles of the political and economic system on which the state rests, and the necessary skills to be a useful and accepted member of the society. So defining education confines the power of the state to its rightful place as the trainer of citizens. Education is thereby demystified as the creator of persons. Does not the concept of democracy include not only separation of church and state but separation of state and person? The citizen belongs to the state; the person belongs to God or the Void, or both.

If education is narrowed to the role of creating citizens, it can be divided then into two parts: knowledge and understanding. Knowledge is comprised of the skills and information needed to subsist and maintain the status quo. Such skills are intellectual, technical, and mechanical. Knowledge is concerned with the tangible: thus it can be taught.

Understanding belongs to the realm of the sacred. It comes, wrote Aldous Huxley in his essay "Knowledge and Understanding," "when we liberate ourselves from the old and so make possible a direct, unmediated contact with the new, the mystery, moment by moment, of our existence." Understanding cannot be taught, because it comes, slowly and painfully, when knowledge has reached its limits and there is still a compelling reason to know. Understanding comes when knowledge intersects experience and is found inadequate.

Understanding provides what mere knowledge cannot — the courage to meet, as adults, the problems of the society. And to meet is not to solve. (The Old English root of *meet* is "conversation.") Knowledge leads to the error of trying to solve problems, and it is an American disease, as Huxley observed, to believe that all problems have solutions.

The faculty of understanding is all we have to converse with the insoluble. It is sufficient for the task.

In 1954, the Supreme Court, through no fault of its own, was unable to meet the problem of white supremacy. However, it had the wisdom and courage to dismantle the major institution in the apparatus of white supremacy.

Since then, the white majority has continued to amaze by its ability to avoid the contradiction that remains at democracy's core — white supremacy. Although it is not fashionable now to use the rhetoric of racial superiority, the rhetoric of moral superiority is seeking to become the law of the land.

As long as the white majority willfully refuses to meet the profound implications of *Brown*, as long as the white majority refuses to learn to live as merely one element in a multiracial, multicultural society, the national identity will remain bound to white supremacy. As long as it does, the nation will be threatened by a majority that considers itself morally superior, because it was a sense of moral superiority that created white supremacy.

Safe Sex

✧✧✧

The motto for the waning years of the twentieth century seems to be Safe Sex. With these words, many colleges and universities justify distributing condoms to students. This appears to be a reasonable and prudent response to the AIDS epidemic, because college students are going to have sex, regardless, so at least make it safe.

Predictably, political and religious conservatives are protesting the wholesale dissemination of condoms. They maintain that sexual promiscuity is being promoted and the nation is taking another step into an immorality that will make the last days of the Roman Empire look like Puritan New England.

There are many of us who remember an archaic time before birth control pills, a time when sexual awakening was stamped with the motto No Sex. Condoms were dispensed from machines in the dirty bathrooms of filling stations and disreputable bars, or slipped to you surreptitiously from under the counter by druggists who looked like John Calvin. And in every neighborhood, there was some unfortunate teenage couple who, despite condoms, found themselves married as expectant parents at age sixteen. In those days, the only safe sex was an active fantasy life.

Perhaps conservatives can be forgiven for wondering why No Sex was a reasonable alternative when unwanted pregnancy might be the consequence of sex, but No Sex is not regarded as a reasonable alternative when death might be the consequence.

It is particularly distressing that colleges and universities are promoting so-called safe sex. The institutions charged with educating the young should know that there is no such thing. If they wish to speak of "disease-free sex," that is one thing. But safe sex?

Our institutions of so-called higher learning are forgetting that sex is not primarily a physical act; it is an emotional one — even, at blessed moments, a spiritual one. The most casual of sexual encounters is emotional because it can inflate the already inflated macho ego of a man, leave a woman feeling used and abused, or suck a participant into a loneliness more piercing than the one from which he or she had thought to flee.

Sex is not safe. It cannot be. When two people who have been married for many years present their nakedness to each other, there is familiarity but not safety. The nakedness is more than physical, for in the sexual act, whatever emotions are present will be felt by the other. Anger, resentment, and boredom are expressed as forcefully as love, joy, and respect when one person stands naked before another.

In the first edition of John Fowles's novel *The Magus*, there are these words:

> We lay on the ground and kissed. Perhaps you smile. That we only lay on the ground and kissed. You young people can lend your bodies now, play with them, give them as we could not. But remember that you have paid a price: that of a world rich in mystery

and delicate emotion. It is not only species of animal that die out. But whole species of feeling. And if you are wise you will never pity the past for what it did not know. But pity yourself for what it did.

To lead the young to believe that sex is safe may one day deprive them of love itself.

Integration

✧✧✧

Despite racism, blacks have been integrated into the American fabric, and in ways that are not flattering.

I am a fanatic sports fan. I take pride in the fact that there is not a ball of any kind hit, thrown, caught, or kicked on television that I don't see. I especially like football and baseball — but I do not cheer for the Cleveland Indians, Kansas City Chiefs, Atlanta Braves, and Washington Redskins. I am hurt, saddened, and angered that black men play for teams with such names and that black fans go to games dressed in full-length Indian headdresses.

If there were a team named the Washington Niggers, those same blacks would be leading the protests outside the stadium. But no one would dare name a team that. Nor would anyone name teams the Dallas Dagos, the Washington Wops, or the Kansas City Kikes. Indians, Redskins, and Chiefs are fine, however.

There is a certain irony in giving teams such nicknames, because less than a hundred years ago, Native American groups were called savages when they defended their lands and lives from invaders. Yet, now that they have been defeated and demoralized, their lands taken, their lives con-

216

trolled by the secretary of the interior, it is as if there is some residual magic in their fighting spirit that can be transferred to the playing field and bring victory.

One year during the pregame show before a Washington-Dallas football game, an interviewer asked the black newspaper columnist Carl Rowan a typically insightful question: "Who are you rooting for?" And Rowan, who regularly excoriates white America for its racism, said loudly, "The Redskins!"

I bowed my head in shame. Yes, blacks have become so thoroughly integrated that they cannot even see it. Carl Rowan should have known better. All blacks should have been so sensitized by our experiences in this country that we can recognize when we are being insensitive to others. I would like to think that civil-rights groups and black athletes would ask the owners of the Washington Redskins, Atlanta Braves, Cleveland Indians, and Kansas City Chiefs to change the team nicknames.

I don't think it will happen, though.

Who said integration was progress?

The Return of the Sixties

❖❖❖

If the protests of the sixties ever return, I will be ready.

I'm going to start a picket-sign business called the Moral Millions. For a mere $4.95, a protester could purchase a picket sign preprinted with words "US Out of" and then there'd be a blank. Into this slot could be inserted the name of the place of your choice — El Salvador, South Africa, Nicaragua, Washington, D.C. Every month or so, I'd offer inserts with the names of new countries so that the conscientious protester would never be caught unprepared or embarrassed by the nefarious machinations of US foreign policy. And not wanting anyone to think that I am an ideologue, I would have my company offer similar picket signs to the other side; these would read "Bomb" and then there'd be a space to insert the name of Russia, China, Los Angeles.

As a survivor of the sixties, I wonder if I am becoming old and cynical. My response to current demonstrations against US involvement in Latin America as well as anti-CIA protests on college campuses is: "Oh, dear. Not again." But I felt that way during the sixties, too.

Does anyone really think he or she is going to stop the CIA from doing what it does? The CIA is not a moral entity, and frankly, I would get a little nervous if it became one.

I'm not opposed to demonstrations, however. Demonstrating is a cheaper and easier way to get high than drugs. But at this point in time, it's not much more than that.

Well, if the sixties do come back, there is no better way to relive them than with one of my All-Purpose Protest Picket Signs. Not only are you freed from having to make a new one for every US transgression, you are also relieved of having to risk misspelling Nicaragua, Zimbabwe, or any other foreign name. For an additional $5, I'll throw in an audiocassette called "Great Demonstrations of the Sixties." Imagine demonstrating outside the White House while listening on your Walkman (should that be Walkperson?) to the sounds of the March on Washington, the 1967 Pentagon demonstration, and the 1968 demonstrations in the streets of Chicago. And, for only $45 more, you can demonstrate in comfort by wearing sneakers designed especially for the serious protestor. This sneaker was designed after months of consultations with sixties protestors, all of whom agreed that if they'd had better footgear, they might be demonstrating still.

I think I'll call it the Self-Righteous Foot.

The Way of All Sharks

❖❖❖

A serious problem has developed in the depths of the ocean. Sharks are biting and rendering inoperative the new fiber-optic cables being laid on the ocean floor. A fiber-optic cable is another one of those technological miracles that we accept as ordinary. Less than an inch in diameter, a cable holds six hairlike strands of glass that can carry as many as forty thousand separate conversations beneath the Atlantic or Pacific oceans.

One shark bite not only disrupts communications, it costs a minimum of $250,000 to repair — sometimes more, depending on the depth at which the cable was laid.

No one is sure why sharks are biting the cables. Could it be that sharks are antitechnology? Are they angry that something alien is being laid across the floor of their living room? I wouldn't be happy to wake up some morning to see sharks laying something across my living-room floor.

Scientists think that vibrations from the cables occur at a frequency sharks identify with food. Sharks are very sensitive to electrical signals and can detect electric fields of a few millionths of a volt per centimeter; such currents trigger an automatic feeding reflex. Cables are now being wrapped in double layers of steel tape and it is hoped that this will solve the problem.

I hope so, because I know how the sharks feel. There are days, many days, when I wonder if I am hearing some faint electrical signal that makes me bare my teeth and bite, though I do not know what I am hearing or why I am biting.

All of us have days, many days, when someone says to us, "What's wrong with you today?" There's nothing wrong that we know of, yet, later, in a moment of reflection, we realize that we have been snapping at people all day, and when we try to find the source of our discontent, we cannot find it.

And then there are the times we meet people and our immediate reaction is that they have "bad vibes," and we bare our teeth and strike. Later, we are ashamed and chide ourselves for being irrational. But perhaps that is not so. Some New Age psychologists maintain that people are little more than vast fields of energy. If that is so, there may indeed be people who emit "bad vibes" and we are powerless to do anything except respond like sharks.

However, we are not only sharks; we are also fiberoptic cables emitting electrical impulses, the "bad vibes" that cause others to attack without any provocation we can identify. I have days when I feel as if my entire body is covered with bite marks and I go to bed muttering, "But I didn't do anything to anybody."

Could the solution to human relationships be something as simple as wrapping ourselves in double layers of steel tape?

Bernhard Goetz

✧✧✧

When a jury found Bernhard Goetz not guilty of attempted murder for shooting four black teenagers on a New York City subway train, black leaders considered the verdict racist, a call to vigilantism and open hunting season on black youth.

Some blacks have suggested that if a black man had shot four white youths, no jury would have declared him not guilty of attempted murder. That is not necessarily so. Recently, a jury in Brooklyn returned a verdict of not guilty in a case in which a young black man murdered a white Catholic priest. In this case, the defense argued that the black man was frightened by the homosexual advances of the priest and, from fear, killed him. That the jury would accept murder as a reasonable response to a homosexual advance reveals an antigay bias far more terrifying than any alleged racial bias in the Goetz case.

Black leaders were guilty of selective memories when they conveniently forgot this case and focused their ire on the Goetz verdict. Their anger at the Goetz verdict was irresponsible because it intensified the divisions between blacks and whites and obfuscated the underlying issue of the Goetz trial.

That issue was fear — black fear and white fear. I wish

that black leaders had the courage to be honest, honest enough to say publicly what we all know: all blacks are not saints. If I were approached by four black youths in a subway car or on the street, I would be foolish to assume that they wanted to discuss the Yankees' chances of winning the pennant. I wish black leaders would be honest and acknowledge that yes, there are black youths who rob and beat and kill and that blacks are as afraid of them as any white person. If I owned a gun and felt that my well-being was threatened, I cannot say that I would not have reacted as did Bernhard Goetz. That is not a justification for what Goetz did or a defense of him; it is merely a simple statement reflecting one of the realities of life in America's cities today. That Bernhard Goetz chose to respond to that reality with gunfire does not necessarily mean he was racist; nor is the jury's verdict a commendation. Goetz's act and the jury's verdict should tell us how deeply afraid we are, how unsafe we feel whenever we venture into public, and how unable we are to protect ourselves.

We are afraid, each and every one of us. Blacks are afraid that there are many Bernhard Goetzes out there, who will now shoot them down on the slightest pretext. That fear is real and must be respected. Whites are afraid that they will be beaten, robbed, or killed by black youths. That fear is also real and must be respected.

We are afraid of each other, blacks and whites. We have no basis on which to trust each other. We regard each other with an active and increasingly deadly mistrust, which can only lead to an open and even more deadly antagonism.

The only way out is to admit our fear of each other. That is not easy, especially in a society as contemptuous of fear as ours. But in acknowledging our fear, we accept our humanity.

Those who condemn or defend Bernhard Goetz dangerously distort what his case means on the most fundamental level — namely, that fear can transform any one of us into a killer.

It is far more healing simply to say, each to the other, "I am afraid."

Aren't you?

Summertime and the Livin' Is —

❖❖❖

Each summer, I find myself confused about something. What I'm confused about is — well — how shall I put it? There's no subtle way to do it. What I'm confused about is white people!

I was in a store recently and it was as if every shelf was filled with bottles and containers of a product for which I have no use: suntan lotion.

I don't understand. For three seasons of the year, there is not the shadow of a doubt in my mind that white people are thrilled that they are not black. I know that is true because of the way black people are regarded and treated in this country. Then, along comes summer and all over the Western world there is the sound of white people taking off every stitch of clothing the law allows, slapping their bodies with oily lotion, and flopping down on the nearest patch of grass or sand. And they lie there. When they get done on one side, they turn over. When evening comes, they go home and everybody says: 'You've got a beautiful tan. You look gorgeous."

I don't understand. There're about thirty million folks of African descent in this country with tans that are even all over, and white folks don't be telling us how gorgeous we look. In fact, they be trying to convince us that we ain't gorgeous.

On the one hand, anybody who lays out in the sun all day obviously does not have both oars in the water. However, you ever take a close look at white people near the end of winter? They be looking like Death sitting on a tombstone eating soda crackers. I mean, if I was white and looked that pale, I'd be laying out in the sun, too — every chance I got.

I guess the truth of the matter is that deep down, way deep down, white folks want to be black. It's impossible to reach any other conclusion seeing how much money they spend and how much effort they put into getting that tan. I mean, have you ever noticed how superior white folks with tans act when they're around white folks that ain't got none? I mean, they even try to get superior with me. A friend of mine who'd spent the previous week broiling on the beach came up to me, put her Coppertone arm next to mine, and said, "I'll be as dark as you pretty soon."

Well, now that I understand that white people really want to be black (and, Lord knows, I can't blame 'em for that), and that the whole source of the race problem is jealousy of how gorgeous we are, the solution is evident and simple.

Therefore, I am putting on the market a special kit called Be Black. For a mere $79.95, you will get a summer's supply of tanning lotion, a sunlamp kit to keep you from looking like the ghost of Christmas past in February, books by Richard Wright and Alice Walker, a "rap" record, an instructional video on how to walk, talk, and slap hands, and, as a bonus, my recipe for fried chicken.

Just imagine! A mere $79.95 from every white person in America will solve America's race problem. And if it doesn't, it'll make me rich enough to move to the mountains of Switzerland, where I can see snow all year round. I can't stand summer!

Video Games

✧✧✧

Oddly, there are people who think video games are a threat to civilization. The town of Irvington, New York, passed an ordinance "to protect the adolescents of the villages against the evils associated with gambling," though gambling is not a part of video games. Mesquite, Texas, has forbidden the playing of video games by anyone under seventeen. And, of course, there are psychologists who have studied the effects of video games on the young and concluded that video games do not encourage relatedness, as if anything else in America did.

I would have an opinion on the subject if I didn't go to video-game arcades at least once a week — sometimes to play, other times to watch others play — because there is no other place in America where children and adults meet as equals, where men in suits, women pushing strollers, and children and adolescents engage in a common enterprise. Kids give adults advice on the best way to play a particular game, and adults get beaten by children at a game and enjoy it.

Video-game arcades are also museums of the imagination in which the infinity of inner space is explored. The games make sounds beyond the ability of the human voice, sounds for an inner ear that may still retain over-tones from the womb. The colors appearing on the screens of the games are the equal of an Impressionist's palette.

Most important are the games themselves. The princi-ple object of most games is shooting something — alien spacecraft, meteors, asteroids, creatures from another world. The sentimental moralists deem this violence.

That it is, and any morality not burdened by sentimen-tality recognizes and accepts that violence is an inescapa-ble part of being human. It is not the existence of violence that is to be condemned, but whether we find ways to me-diate that violence within ourselves before we inflict it on ourselves and others.

In a real sense, each of us is alone in space, trying to pilot our tiny spacecraft safely through falling asteroids and meteors as we find ourselves being transgressed upon by aliens of one kind or another — the landlord, a neigh-bor, spouses, children, or the jerk driving too fast on an icy street.

So when I stand next to my son and watch him coolly playing a video game — his right hand calmly guiding his spaceship up and down to avoid enemy gunfire, meteors, and asteroids, while his left hand fires laser beams at the other alien objects seeking to invade his space and destroy his frail craft — and as I see his score mount to 40,000 or 50,000, I can't help feeling that, yes, maybe, just maybe, he will be able to meet with confidence all the creatures of inner space awaiting him.

Video games are visual representations of psychic real-ity. They are fairy tales of our time, and my son is Prince Charming.

Rosh Hashanah Is Not "Happy New Year"

✧✧✧

I don't like it when gentile and Jewish friends greet me at Rosh Hashanah with "Happy New Year." Rosh Hashanah is not the Jewish equivalent of January 1.

I have never understood what "Happy New Year" is supposed to mean. I've never been sure that I want to be wished happiness. I'm not sure I know what happiness is, or that it is as important as we think. Happiness *feels* better than misery, but some of the most significant periods of my life have been the ones of profound unhappiness. For all the feelings of well-being that happiness bestows upon us, it is not the goal of life.

The appropriate greeting for Rosh Hashanah is *La Shana Tova u-metukah tikateiva:* "May you be inscribed for a sweet and good year." This is very different from "Happy New Year." I might well spend the next year totally depressed, but that may be where I need to be in my life — which would mean, then, that I did have a good and sweet year. That it felt otherwise is not important.

Rosh Hashanah is an amazing period, which is why the ten days between Rosh Hashanah and Yom Kippur are called Yamim Noraim, "Days of Awe." On the first day of Rosh Hashanah, I come out of synagogue between one-thirty and two o'clock. I have been there since services began at eight-thirty that morning. As I walk away, I notice the postman crossing the synagogue lawn. It takes a moment to recognize what he is, and another moment to remember that, for him, it is merely another day of work.

A little later, I notice children returning from school and I feel as if I am looking at a movie in which I have little interest. Someone asks me, "What day is today?" and he or she is also in that dimension called Rosh Hashanah, a dimension so encompassing that the world as we knew it a mere twenty-four hours ago no longer exists.

That evening, I realize that I have not heard the news all day, have not read a newspaper, don't know who won or who lost in the previous night's baseball games. Most surprising is that I don't care. Then I understand what makes Rosh Hashanah different from the New Year of January 1. That space in time called Rosh Hashanah, a space that really encompasses ten days, has the power to renew those who enter it. It is a time of withdrawal from the world in order to renew one's love for the world.

There is another aspect to Rosh Hashanah. It is also known as *hayom harat olam* — "the birthday of the world." During Rosh Hashanah, we withdraw from the world in order to enter it more deeply by becoming conscious of who we are and what our relationship to the world has been during the previous year. It is a way of celebrating the world, not by blowing noisemakers and getting drunk but by taking responsibility for who we are in the world, because, in the deepest sense, we *are* the world.

How incredible it would be if once a year, for ten days, the world would close up for real. The television and radio stations would go off the air; newspapers would stop publishing; stores and businesses would close and everyone would observe the birthday of the world by examining what he or she had done to the world over the previous year.

Happy birthday, world! I'm going to try real hard to treat you better than I did last year.

Pollution in Space

✧✧✧

Will we ever mature as a nation? I have my doubts. One characteristic of maturity is the ability to anticipate a problem and take action to prevent it. Is that maturity or plain common sense? Whichever it is, the nation is without it.

In Cheyenne Mountain, Colorado, there is an Air Force captain named David P. Boyarski who has an unusual job. From nine to five every day, he keeps track of and identifies space debris.

Having polluted the environment of Earth to a critical point, we are now busy polluting space. Captain Boyarski's job is to monitor nearly seven thousand orbiting objects, everything from dead satellites and spent rocket engines to an astronaut's wrench and thousands of whirling fragments from more than ninety satellites and rockets. These seven thousand pieces of junk are only the ones closest to Earth. In reality, there are millions of tiny bits of junk whirling and floating in space, some of them as high as 23,000 miles. These include flecks of paint from rockets and spaceships.

The problem is serious. The most obvious aspect is that space junk is a danger to satellites and spaceships. In 1983, a fleck of paint hit the window of the space shuttle

233

Challenger and left a tiny crater in the window. In July 1987, a Soviet satellite exploded mysteriously, giving rise to the suspicion that it was hit by space debris.

Space debris is interfering with astronomers' telescopes and distorting photographs of stars and galaxies. One recent astronomical "discovery" was later shown to be sunlight reflecting off a piece of orbiting space junk.

Captain Boyarski's job is crucial because he is trying to establish the orbit of each of the seven thousand pieces of space junk so he can predict its path when it eventually falls to Earth. This way it will not be mistaken for an enemy missile and fired upon. Wouldn't the ultimate irony be if World War III started over a wrench falling from space to Earth?

The Sierra Club has issued a book called *Beyond Spaceship Earth: Environmental Ethics and the Solar System*. It is doubtful, however, that anyone involved in the space program of the United States or that of the Soviet Union will read it. Current US thinking about space debris is that cleaning up space would be too expensive, so NASA is designing space vehicles with armor, as if that is a solution to the problem.

Maybe we do not deserve the planet and solar system that were put into our keeping. If someone treats a dog with the thoughtless cruelty shown the Earth and space, the dog is eventually taken away from that person. That is what's going to happen with the Earth and the solar system — except that it is we who are taking them away from ourselves.

Could anything else be expected? A mature nation is not brought into being by a legislative act. A mature nation is the responsibility of each of us, for a mature nation exists only when there are mature citizens.

I'm not sure I know what a mature citizen is, but, at the very least, a mature citizen is one who lives in grateful awe of the heavens above and the Earth beneath.

Rainmaker

✧✧✧

Dateline Kampala, Uganda:

Ugandan villagers have beaten their local rainmaker to death, blaming him for hailstorms and torrential rains, travelers from the southwest reported today. After weather devastated crops and homes in the Kabale-district last week, the travelers said, the villagers turned on the rainmaker, Festo Kazarwa, because he had threatened to summon up hailstorms unless people showed him more respect.

My first response on reading this article from a *New York Times* of late autumn 1987 was laughter. How else can someone of Western sensibilities respond? We are a decade away from the twenty-first century and there's a village in Uganda that has a rainmaker? I realize that there are different brands of New Age folk harmonically converged on a tofu stand in Colorado who believe in rainmakers and witches. But for the rest of us, the new age is middle age and the closest thing to a harmonic convergence we know of is Häagen-Dazs vanilla ice cream. Such a news item serves to confirm white Westerners in their cultural superiority, because what better proof could there be that Africa is as primitive and superstitious as the Tarzan movies claimed. But everybody knows black people are strange, regardless of the continent they live on. Who else but somebody black would carry around a fifty-pound radio, turn the volume up high enough to cause tall buildings to shake, and then put the radio on his shoulder, right next to his ear? If black people in America do something like that, you really can't be surprised that on the continent from which black folks came people still beat rainmakers to death.

After I stopped laughing, I found myself envying people who believe so deeply in rainmakers that they beat one to death. I live in a country where most believe that the individual is powerless to affect the course of human events; and certainly, few Americans believe that an individual can command the powers of nature.

And yet, in a village in Uganda, there are people who do not think of themselves as inconsequential and impotent, people who believe that one person can cause hailstorms and torrential rains. I envy them their belief even as their belief frightens me. After all, in Renaissance Europe and Colonial America, thousands of people, most of them women, were burned at stakes because people believed these individuals had such powers.

Frightened or not, I take no solace in my desire to ridicule those Ugandans who believe in rainmakers. In fact, I ask myself, is there something missing from me that I do *not* believe in rainmakers? Am I the one living in an underdeveloped country — a country that teaches me that I am not equal to creation, a country that teaches me to believe nothing that can't be proven, a country that teaches me to have contempt for others who do not believe as we in America believe, a country that teaches me to ridicule those who believe in rainmakers?

Deep down, I guess, I would like to be a rainmaker. Deep down, I would like all of us to be so firmly rooted in creation and in ourselves that we could all be rainmakers. But you can be a rainmaker only if you believe, really believe that you matter.

Who Are You after You Quit Smoking?

✧✧✧

I quit smoking. It wasn't easy, and if it had not been for an individualized program of acupuncture, I doubt that I could have gotten through those first two months, when dying of lung cancer seemed infinitely more attractive than the pain of withdrawal.

But my body has stopped begging for nicotine. Oh, there are moments when I see someone light up and my being swoons with memories of that deep first drag on a cigarette. But then I remember, too, the feelings of shame at my inability to function without a cigarette and I am glad to be free. There are other times when I watch someone light up and I'm glad I am not that person. The most interesting times are those when I am with someone who smokes and I am indifferent to their cigarettes. Those are the moments of real freedom.

Stopping smoking is like going through a divorce. I smoked for thirty-two years. My relationship to cigarettes qualifies as the most enduring of my life. For thirty-two years, cigarettes were my constant companion, an intimate, a confidant that never let me down.

I did not know until I stopped how much of my identity

238

was involved in being a smoker. Long after the physical craving for tobacco passed, I didn't know who I was. I used to walk into restaurants and say, "Smoking section," with real pride. Now I don't know what to say. I would prefer to be with the smokers because that is who I was from age seventeen. But I am not a smoker anymore.

Neither am I an ex-smoker. That is still defining myself in relationship to cigarettes. I need to know who or what I am without a celluloid image of Humphrey Bogart or Edward G. Robinson — cigarette dangling from the corner of his mouth — flashing onto my inner movie screen. Certainly, one of the reasons I became a smoker as a teen was that I associated cigarettes with maleness. But there is another association. Remember a movie of the early sixties called *Hiroshima, Mon Amour?* It was a film in which the hero and heroine made love a lot and afterward smoked many cigarettes, and the act of smoking seemed more fulfilling than the lovemaking.

There is something in me that feels unfulfilled now that I am no longer a smoker. There are ways in which I am no longer familiar to myself and must ask, yet again, who am I?

I think the answer may be horrifyingly simple: I am me, and I could not say that as long as I was dominated by the craving for tobacco.

The most gratifying experience I've had since I stopped has been the response of those I know. I don't think I've ever received so many warm congratulations or heard so many shouts of exultation.

I never knew that my smoking mattered to them, which is a way of saying that I didn't know that I mattered to them.

And maybe that's what stopping smoking is — a way of saying to myself that I matter.

Lester for President

✧✧✧

I have decided to run for president of the United States. That the American electorate will respond to this announcement with a big yawn is no surprise. That is how the electorate responds when anybody announces that he or she is running.

Many, of course, will wonder, "Who is Julius Lester and what makes him think he should be president?" But that is what they have said about all the others so eager to lead us into the greater tomorrow. Thus, by merely announcing my candidacy, I am on an equal footing with other presidential candidates.

Now we come to the more critical issue — my qualifications. Presidential candidates are usually congresspeople, governors, or vice-presidents. What are my qualifications for the presidency?

This is where I have a distinct advantage over anyone else who may run. I have no qualifications! None whatsoever! I have never held elective office, served on a government commission, or been appointed to any official boards or cabinet positions. I did not defend my country in any of its wars. In fact, I was IV-F and proud of it. I have never coached Little League and I think kissing the babies of strangers is sick. I did receive the key to the city

240

of Memphis once, but since the city isn't locked, what good is the key? And to be frank, if Memphis was locked and I had the key, I wouldn't unlock it. But that's another story.

My lack of qualifications is brilliant, and it doesn't end there. I am not a registered voter. I was once and I voted for Lyndon Johnson, and I figured if I was going to use my vote like that, I might as well stay home on Election Day. In addition to the above, I do not have a degree from Harvard Law School, or any law school. In fact, I don't have any kind of degree from Harvard, and on that basis alone I should probably carry the South, the Midwest, the Mountain States, and the Virgin Islands. To round out this distinguished listing of ineptitude and civic indifference, not only am I black, I am also Jewish. When you add up all these liabilities, there can no longer be a doubt in your mind that I am the best candidate for president, equally unqualified to lead the country back to the eighteenth century or forward to the twenty-first. Under me, the country would go absolutely nowhere, and that's a promise!

After many years of intense study of American history and the presidency, I have concluded that we Americans have consistently made the same mistake — namely, time after time, we elect as president men we consider qualified for the office, men with years of service as governors and senators. Look at what these qualified men have done: spent billions on weapons, subverted governments all around the world, been incapable of stopping drug trafficking, done nothing to decrease poverty or deliver health-care services to those most in need of them. These qualified men have brought us acid rain, holes in the ozone layer, and a missile for every garage.

Obviously, the time has come to put in the White House someone who is highly unqualified. We couldn't be any worse off.

Holidays

✧✧✧

When I was a kid, Memorial Day was May 30. Lincoln's Birthday was February 12 and Washington's was February 22, and we didn't go to school on either. In the fall, there was Columbus Day on October 12 and Armistice Day, marking the end of World War I, on November 11.

What I remember about those days is not their historical meaning, but something more important. What I remember is the pause in the week, that strange Wednesday or Thursday when there weren't many cars on the streets and no stores were open and everyone moved more slowly and it was like Sunday and for the rest of the week you had trouble remembering what day it was.

There was an almost total suspension of activity on a day when ordinarily there was activity. The hiatus was accentuated because there were no newspapers on those midweek holidays. I didn't understand how the people at newspapers knew nothing significant was going to happen on a holiday, but nothing ever did. On a holiday, even the news wasn't important.

There were no baseball or football games to watch on television because there was no television. Neither was there a Dan Rather, Tom Brokaw, or Peter Jennings to re-

242

mind us of that world whose woes we were relieved not to be reminded of for one day.

That was the meaning of those holidays. They were days of being outside the time of routine tasks and duties and worries. They were days of quiet, outer and inner. They were holidays in the original sense of the word — that is, they were holy days, because holiness is uncovered when dailiness is put in the closet. When we enter holiness, we rediscover ourselves and each other.

It's not like that anymore. Holidays are not observed on their calendar day but on specific Mondays, so that we can have three-day weekends. A three-day weekend is convenient and efficient but it is not the shocking surprise of holiness.

We have traded holiness for convenience; we have exchanged a day out of time for the ordinary time we already have too much of. And in the evening, we watch the television news and are shown the pictures of parades in Ohio, and we listen to excerpts from the speeches of politicians and smile at a Charles Kuralt story about some old lady in West Virginia who every year for the past eighty-seven years has gone out on this holiday and spoon-fed red-white-and-blue yogurt to a moose who can recite the Gettysburg Address. And the next day at work we say to each other, "How was your holiday?" and we answer heartily, "Great!"

But a holiday is not just a day off from work. It is the opportunity to participate in holiness and remember that we are other than and more than wage earners and consumers. It is becoming more and more difficult to know that, especially because holidays are no longer noted for the suspension of time or for the unexpected and welcome quiet. No. As any good American knows, holidays mean only one thing now: sale days at the mall.

The Cultural Canon

❖❖❖

In the present debates over the cultural canon and what should constitute it, what we have, in reality, is a rather interesting power struggle. What is at stake is whether or not those who define themselves as victims are going to be permitted to come in from the cold. What we have is a plea for acceptance by blacks and women under the guise of demands for a more inclusive and less Eurocentric curriculum.

At first glance this appears reasonable. After all, there is sufficient evidence to prove that many of those who gave us the cultural canon deliberately suppressed knowledge about blacks and women. The historical moment has arrived when such knowledge must be returned to its rightful place of respect; and in so doing, our ideas of what constitutes the cultural canon must, of necessity, change.

It is assumed that such change will be for the better. How could it not be if those who were excluded are now to be included? Change is not, however, necessarily good simply because it is change. Requiring students to study Asian, African, or Latin American history does not automatically make for a more well educated person. It can create a more well informed bigot.

I fear that those seeking to redress the Eurocentrism of the cultural canon may succeed only in narrowing our vision of what it is to be human. Many of us in academia encounter this when young feminist students question the integrity of a course because there are no books by women on the reading list, or not enough by their definition. We encounter it when black students question a professor's qualifications to teach black literature or history because that professor is white.

Underlying the effort to change the cultural canon is an attitude that has been prevalent since the late sixties — the attitude that says that only someone who has experience in the flesh is qualified to speak, write, and teach about certain topics. Thus, there are feminists who question whether a male writer, because he is male, can have anything of value to say about women. There are blacks who consider the classics of Western civilization irrelevant because "they do not speak to my experience as a black person," as I have heard it expressed.

While the intent may be to balance the curriculum, what appears to be happening is the canonization of difference. What appears to be happening is that we are no longer willing to speak with confidence about something called the human experience. Instead, we have retreated to forts in the wilderness called the black experience, the gay experience, women's experience. There are feminists who contend that men respond to literature differently than women do. Elaine Showalter of Princeton was quoted in the *New York Times Magazine* (June 5, 1988) as saying that what is needed is a "defamiliarization of masculinity, . . . a poetics of the Other." (Perhaps what is needed first is an attitude of mercy toward the English language.)

The black experience and women's experience are spoken of as if they are unique, so distinctive that they bear no resemblance to the experiences of nonblacks or men. The black experience and women's experience are presented as if they are as exclusive as a fashionable country club that admits its members only by virtue of birth: if you are not born black or female, then it is impossible for you to understand what it is like to be black or female.

This attitude correlates collective identity with intellectual and emotional perception and comes dangerously close to equating biology with human values. Because I was born into a particular race or gender, the argument goes, I have direct experience and knowledge unavailable to those not of my race or gender. (Among the few experiences about which that can be said incontrovertibly are menstruation and childbirth.) Notions of genetic superiority seem to be recognizable when their source is white males but less so when blacks or women subtly put them forth.

Many black and many female students today enter the classroom expecting, demanding, that the professor and the course be a mirror that gives them a perfect reflection of themselves. When I do not do this, a young woman in the class usually will inform me that something I have said represents "a man's point of view."

And what, precisely, is that? I want to know. But many feminists today assume that there exists something called a man's point of view; that, by definition, the male point of view is wrong; and that no man is capable of saying anything that is not a collective opinion reflecting his gender.

Indeed, one of the disturbing characteristics of our era is that the intellect has been collectivized as surely as farms in Russia under Stalin. The black experience and women's experience are collective concepts, statements of group identity that tend to deny there is something of the individual that exists above and apart from collective definitions. In the past two decades, the value of the individual has been increasing abrogated.

I grew up in the South in the forties and fifties, attended segregated schools, and, in 1956, entered Fisk University, a black college in my hometown of Nashville, Tennessee. During the first two years at Fisk, all students were required to take the same courses — a curriculum that today would constitute the cultural and literary canon extolled by Allan Bloom but considered anathema by many others. So, I took two semesters of Western Civilization, two of American History, and two years of Great Books, starting with the dialogues of Plato and moving on to *Oedipus Rex, Antigone, The Divine Comedy,* Shakespeare, Rousseau, Voltaire, and so on. There was not a black or woman writer among them. Neither I or anyone else noticed. What I noticed and what I remember is the excitement I felt in being guided by my teachers into the world of ideas. In Socrates' discourses about love, I found new ways to think about the complexities and dimensions of that complicated emotion which had me in a continuous state of confusion and agitation. I do not understand how a black student today can think that Plato does not speak to the black experience, unless black people do not experience love. Or am I now to believe that because a person is black, he or she experiences love in a way that is qualitatively different from anyone who has ever existed on the planet?

I remember sitting in Western Civ — 8:00 AM, Tuesdays, Thursdays, and Saturdays — and being overwhelmed by the fact that so much had taken place before I made *my* entrance into history. I never sorted out the Hundred Years' War from the Wars of the Roses, and what's more, I didn't care about them. But so what? Every event in human history does not have to relate to my personal experience, and isn't it arrogant to think that that which does not relate directly to me is irrelevant? This is collective narcissism.

I went through four years of college and was not taught about blacks or Africa or women. My education did not reflect, confirm, or confer black identity on me. But it was not supposed to. The conferring of identity is a task that belongs to the individual and the group or groups of which he or she is a part.

However, higher education has always had an air of religious salvation about it. In times past, a degree from certain schools confirmed one's identity as a gentleman. Now, it appears that it is important that one be graduated from college with the imprimatur of being politically correct. That is why those who challenge Eurocentrism in higher education are not changing anything except the titles of the books. The center of cultural narcissism remains undisturbed.

The function of education is not to confirm us in who we are; it is to introduce us to all that we are not. Education should overwhelm us to such an extent that we will never again assume that *our* experience, as individuals or as part of a collective, can be equated with human experience. In other words, education should impress us with how vast creation is and how small we are in the midst of it; and in the acceptance of that is the beginning of wisdom.

My education did not confirm me as a black man; it confirmed me as one who had the same questions as Plato and Aristotle. And my education told me that as a black person, it was not only all right to ask those questions, it was even okay to put forward my own answers and stand them next to those of Plato and Aristotle. The cultural canon was presented to me in such a way that I was thrust into that vast and complex mystery which life is; and I graduated from college with an intense and passionate curiosity, which led me to study that which my formal education had omitted — namely, black history and literature and women's history and much, much more.

It is the function of education to introduce the student to the terrifying unknown and provide not only the intellectual skills to make known the unknown but the emotional stability to withstand the terror when the unknown cannot be made known. Such an experience gives the student the self-confidence to go forth and face that mystery which lies at the core of each of us: Who am I?

Something called "the black experience" or "women's experience" is no comfort in the middle of the night when our souls stare at us with unblinking eyes. But we put on collective identities and flaunt them because we are terrified of the loneliness of the journey required to fashion an identity that will make us uniquely us.

To the extent that we exploit differences and use differences to push others away, to the extent that we use differences to make ourselves impregnable to others, we commit violence against the human spirit. It is reprehensible that those who have suffered because they are different should now be the ones using difference as a weapon against others. Doing so denies that we are bound to each other by the simple fact that we all laugh and we all cry, we all suffer and we all rejoice; and it does not matter whether we all laugh and cry and suffer and rejoice about the same experiences or in the same ways. What matters is that we find the humanity within ourselves to delight in the laughter of others, even if we are not amused; that we feel a twinge of pain upon noticing someone weeping, though our own eyes remain dry; that our hearts pause in the presence of another person's suffering; and that we exult when someone else rejoices, even when we do not understand the occasion for the joy.

What matters, then, is not the canon — not what books we read. What matters is the attitude we bring to the canon. Gertrude Himmelfarb has written that "it used to be thought that ideas transcend race, gender and class, that there are such things as truth, reason, morality and artistic excellence, which can be understood and aspired to by everyone, of whatever race, gender or class."

I still believe in truth and beauty and do not believe that a work or idea is invalid by definition because its creator is white and male. I still believe that knowledge and creativity are the birthright of humanity and not the exclusive property of a portion of humanity, be that portion white, male, black, or female.

Ultimately, what constitutes the cultural canon may not matter as much as the quality of the humanity teacher and student bring to the study of that canon.

Caring for the Dead

✧✧✧

On a recent trip to New York City, I spent a day at the Metropolitan Museum of Art. I journeyed from temples of Assyria and pharaonic Egypt to friezes from Greece and Rome to sculptures and masks from Africa and Oceania to the shattering madness of van Gogh to what I, at least, consider the insipidities of much of contemporary American art.

But I found myself returning to ancient Egypt — to the wall paintings from pyramids and the artifacts taken from those tombs. I stood and I stared, but, as hard as I tried, I could not feel that I knew what it was like to live then. What emotions gave rise to the paintings of winged Isis? What feelings did the statues of baboons evoke in those who worshiped them?

I was seeking a foreign remnant of my own humanity, and perhaps I did not find it because I was also troubled. When I came to the mummy cases, I found myself passing them by, unable or unwilling to look, and I knew then why I was troubled. All that I had been looking at had been taken from tombs. All I was seeing belonged to the realm of the dead, and I couldn't help but feel that I was violating something or someone.

251

I was reminded of my day at the Metropolitan Museum when I heard a case before a court in Kenya. S. M. Otieno was a successful Kenyan lawyer, and thoroughly Western. He drove a Mercedes, liked to watch "Perry Mason" on his VCR, enjoyed reciting Shakespeare to friends, and sent his children to schools in Britain and the United States. But on December 20, 1986, when he died of hypertension (a sign of how Western he had become), his wife was prevented from burying him on his country farm. Why? Attorney Otieno was born into the Luo tribe, and the tribe went to court to plead that if Otieno was not given a traditional burial in his tribal homeland, his spirit would haunt the survivors. One Luo commented that already Otieno had been haunting them because he had been buried wearing a necktie: "He screams that the tie is choking him."

Well, I can relate to that. Bury me in a tie and see if I don't make everybody's life miserable.

At any rate, the widow argued that her husband never visited his tribal homeland, did not teach his children the language, and wished to be buried at his farm. "Tribe is a natural connection," the lawyer for the tribe responded. "You can become British, but you can't become English." The court agreed and ordered that attorney Otieno be buried in Luoland.

There is something compelling in knowing that somewhere in the world, there is not a barrier between the realms of the living and the dead — that somewhere in the world, people go to court and argue that life does not end merely because the body ceases to be a self-sustaining organism.

That is what I sensed among the artifacts of ancient Egypt, and as grateful as I am for that wonderful museum and the opportunity to see objects and images I could not otherwise, I felt restless spirits there, resentful of my intrusion, angry that objects and images necessary for the journey of their soul had become mere art, an aesthetic experience for the liberally educated.

I hope those spirits will forgive me and forgive us all for our ignorance and callousness, forgive us for not knowing that life does not end with death but encompasses it in the same way that death encompasses life.

Perhaps we in American society do such a poor job of caring for the living because we do not know how to care for the dead.

The Stone That Weeps

❖❖❖

It is a summer day, any summer day, 1944. I stare into memory but I see no pictures of what I did on any of those days that summer. I suppose I did what any five-year-old does. And whatever that is, there was less of it for a five-year-old black child in Kansas City, Kansas, in 1944.

It is a summer day, any summer day, 1944. I do not know there is a place called Europe and that all across the continent five-year-old Jewish children are being murdered.

I could not have known. I was only five. Somehow that does not matter. If knowledge is limited to that which we have experienced personally, we are all named Narcissus.

But knowledge is not synonymous with the subjective. Knowledge and experience also include the impersonal. An airplane crashes halfway around the world and tears fill my eyes because someone's child was on that plane; because I am a parent, I do not have to know the name of the child to feel the grief of a parent. (The bell always tolls for me if I am listening for it.)

During the first six years of my life, I did not know that something was being done to me on the bodies of Jewish children. Now I know that I am alive and so many are not who should be.

Though I was only a child, I am struck by guilt. Perhaps it is because after Auschwitz, innocence is not possible. I am alive. So many are not who should be. Innocence can be no more. I cannot permit myself the charming irresponsibility of thinking that it should be otherwise. I cannot permit myself to assume that by definition — because I am black, because I am a Jew — I belong with those who involuntarily went to heaven through the chimneys of crematoriums. To be innocent is to believe that because I am Jew, because I am black, I am by definition victim and am therefore exempt from being executioner.

Thus, my guilt has two faces: I am alive because I happened to be born black in the United States rather than Jewish in Europe; and because I am alive, I am guilty to the extent that I deceive myself into believing that the victim cannot also be executioner. I am guilty to the extent that I look at the Holocaust and insist on my innocence, for to be innocent is to deceive myself about what it means to be human.

2 ✧✧✧

I cannot remember when I first became aware of the Holocaust. I suppose it was the fall of 1957, the beginning of my sophomore year at Fisk University in Nashville, Tennessee. Rhoda Miller, a classmate, thrust a book at me and said imperiously, "Read this."

The book was *Exodus* by Leon Uris. I do not remember one scene from the novel and I refuse to go to my bookshelf, take down my copy, and leaf through its pages to see if any memories come back after more than three decades.

For me, the Holocaust is not contained in or embodied by specific images created by passages in books or remembered from still photographs or films. It is more pervasive than that.

I read *Exodus* at age eighteen and was transformed. It is similar to what happens after you are married a certain number of years, or after the birth of a child. You know that you had a life before you were married, before you had this particular child, but you cannot remember what that life was or how you could have thought it had meaning. Most odd are those times you turn to your wife and say, "Remember when we saw such-and-such a movie," and she doesn't remember, and you persist, recalling the restaurant where you ate, and she still recalls nothing. Suddenly, you remember: you saw the movie before you met her who now sits across from you, and, in fact, you were with whatever-her-name-was that night. So fully has your life been absorbed into marriage that your wife's presence has infiltrated and claimed periods of your biography that are not hers.

Does it really matter, then, when I or anyone first encountered the Holocaust? Whatever life we had is swallowed whole and ingested by the metaphor of Auschwitz. It is as if it was always there, as if I knew about it from the instant of conception and the first word I spoke was not "Momma" but "Auschwitz." That is not objective reality, of course, but that was how it felt that autumn of my sophomore year, and feeling is a reality that forces the objective to conform to its needs.

It is my junior year, spring 1959. I am attending San Diego State College for a semester, and among my three roommates is a Palestinian named Khalid Tuck-Tuck.

I am assigned the top bunk over his lower one, and perhaps it is for this reason that Tuck and I are supposed to be friends. But, very quickly, I know that I do not want to be his friend. He is obsessed with Jews, and at least once a day, something makes him angry and he blames the

Jews. Often, he talks about the orange trees around his family's home in Jaffa and how beautiful they were until the Jews came and kicked his family out of their home; and then, he cries.

It is an act I soon weary of, and I try to ignore him. One day, in the midst of one of his tirades against Jews, I hear him say, "I wish Hitler had finished what he started."

I am not aware that I am humming until Tuck screams at me, "I hate that song!"

I listen. I am humming "Hava Nagila," which I have heard at a local coffee shop. I hum it louder and the next thing I know, Tuck's hands are around my throat. Our roommates pull him off me.

Oddly, he and I are close friends after that. But he never talks about Jews around me; I never hum "Hava Nagila" around him.

The following spring, I find myself approaching the moment of graduation with no idea of what I want to do with my life. On the first Sunday in June, I will be granted my bachelor's degree in English and exhorted to go forth and conquer the world. All I want is to know who I am.

It is a month or two before that fateful Sunday. I am sitting in the International Student Center, listening to a short, stocky woman with a European accent talk about some girl named Anne Frank.

Dr. Rosey Poole is Dutch and Anne Frank was a Dutch Jewish girl who wrote a diary that Dr. Poole has translated. Although Dr. Poole is not a Jew, she was part of the Dutch resistance and her parents were murdered by the Nazis.

As I listen to her talk about a child hiding in an attic, my imagination topples from its perch like a boulder on a mountainside dislodged by unseen stresses from the earth's core. I understand her accented words, but they don't make sense. I don't know how to live with the knowledge of such evil and such suffering.

A few days later, I sit on the side porch of Robert Hayden's house. He is a poet and teaches creative writing, Victorian literature, and early-twentieth-century American literature. "What did you think of Rosey Poole's talk?" he asks me.

What am I supposed to say? It was good? I enjoyed it? "It's hard to believe," I say finally.

"We think we know something about suffering," he says, referring to black people. "We don't know what suffering means." His protruding eyes peer at me intently through the thick lenses of his glasses as he lights his pipe and puffs at it strenuously until the tobacco glows red. "Well, that's not entirely true. Maybe it's a problem of language." He chuckles. "But that's always the problem, isn't it?" There is a long silence. "Maybe I'm not comfortable using the same word, 'suffering,' to describe what we have gone through and what the Jews went through. Do you know what I mean?"

I did. I had ridden in the backs of buses all my life, had read signs telling me where I could and could not eat, what doors I could and could not go through, what water fountains I could and could not drink from. I had been trained by my parents not to look at white women. Then, I thought about living in an attic and about gas chambers and furnaces into which human beings were shoveled like wastepaper.

"I'm not saying that Jews have suffered more. How can you measure what a human being suffers? But there is a difference, and we need a word to make that difference clear." He chuckles. "Are you still sure you want to be a writer? That's what writing is, you know. Finding the right word."

I would like to be the one to find the right word, to find that word which would crush people and make them understand what it was like to be a Jew in Europe during those years. But is there a word strong enough to hold naked bodies stacked in hills beneath a sunny sky? Being forced to ride at the back of a bus is not in the same realm of experience.

But Jews had to wear yellow Stars of David on their clothes to be identified as Jews. My star is my skin color. Yet, I am alive. Anne Frank is not.

We sit on his side porch, relaxing in the languid and heavy beauty of spring in Nashville, Tennessee. We sit and we talk about Jews being killed in Europe, and I begin to feel unreal. The city of Nashville is undergoing a revolution and I am not part of it.

Since February, students from Fisk and the other black colleges have been demonstrating to desegregate the lunch counters and restaurants downtown. I have not sat in at even a single lunch counter and I am ashamed.

Why do I rage over and mourn for murdered European Jews as I never have for my own people? I want to ask Mr. Hayden, but I am afraid that he will not understand any more than I do.

I still do not understand — but what is it I think should be understood? Is it so strange and unusual and out-of-the-ordinary for a young black to feel that the Holocaust was an experience on such a scale that it requires a response exceeding any you would give to your own people?

Ah! There's the rub. We are taught in America to care for our own first and most. We are taught that the other guy's problems are his problems: take care of your own and don't worry about anybody else.

So, I felt guilty because, compared to Anne Frank, I was

fortunate. Despite segregation, despite racism, despite all the negative experiences that would come to me because I was black, I was alive and so many my age were not who should have been. Was I forbidden to mourn for them because all my sorrow and grief was supposed to be reserved for those who were black like me?

I could not help myself. So many my age were dead who should not have been and, except for an accident of birth, I could have been one of them.

3 ✧✧✧

When Rabbi Hanina the Great came up from Babylon, he wanted to know when he reached Israel, so he picked up stones as he walked, weighing them in his hands. As long as they were light, he said, "I have not yet arrived in Israel." Eventually, the stones were heavy in his hands and he said, "These can only be the stones of the land of Israel." And he kissed them and quoted: "For your servants have desired its stones."

I used to think of my soul as a bird with broad wings that could hold the tiniest wisp of wind. But I was young then, a Peter Pan in danger of disappearing behind the third star to the left as I went toward an eternal morning of perpetual promise.

Now I am older, and I know better: My soul is a stone, broken from that mountain of pain that my ancestor, the Old African, knew when he felt the rough boards of the slave ship beneath his shackled feet, when he looked for the last time at the landscape of the African coast and knew he would never see it again. (When I go to Africa and lift the stones, will I know when I come to the land from which the Old African was stolen?)

My soul is a stone — black, with a texture as rough as

scars that never healed, as heavy as the sobbing that can never be quieted.

But how do you lift a stone that weeps? You can't, not until you open your ears and listen to the crying.

Inside me, there is a crying that wails hysterically as I remember a childhood destroyed by fear. I remember the violence hurling itself at me every time I rode a bus and could not understand why I was not "good" enough to sit anywhere I wanted. I remember not knowing why I was not "good" enough to eat at a lunch counter or restaurant, or why, at gas stations, there was a separate restroom for "Colored" (sometimes it was the field of weeds behind a pile of old tires). I remember that survival meant never looking a white man in the eye, never looking a white woman anywhere, and always saying "Yes, sir" and "Yes, ma'am."

I also remember another pain. But how can I remember that which did not happen to me? Why does it feel as if I remember Auschwitz when my body does not carry memories of its mud, when my nostrils did not inhale the odor of burning flesh, when my eyes have not seen the glow of the crematoriums against the night?

Could it be that memory is not only sensory and I am not only I?

The summer of 1961, I move to New York City. My first job is as a counselor at a camp in the Catskills. I do not know that the camp is what might be considered a progressive, Jewish one: the majority of the campers are the sons and daughters of Jews who grew up listening to Paul Robeson and Pete Seeger records, Jews for whom union songs and Woody Guthrie songs were liturgical chants.

Within a week, I am calling people *meshugge*, referring to the camp food as *trayf*, and muttering *oy gevalt* under my breath. I fall in love with a fellow counselor, a large-eyed Jewish girl with long, dark hair who tells me stories about her grandparents fleeing Russia and invites me into her childhood through borscht, bagels, lox, sour cream and herring, and gefilte fish.

At night, I sit in the camp dining room with the campers, playing my guitar and singing spirituals and songs from the civil-rights movement, which is little more than a year old. They sing Jewish and Israeli songs. I don't know or understand the words, but the melodies sound familiar, and instinctively I seem to know the odd intervals they proceed with. The simplest Israeli song — "Shalom Chaverim" or "Every Man 'Neath His Vine and Fig Tree" — brings tears to my eyes as spirituals never have.

Perhaps that is when I first see myself standing in a synagogue singing Kol Nidre. The centuries of black suffering merge with the millennia of Jewish suffering as my voice weaves the two into a seamless oneness that is the suffering and, at the same time, the only appropriate and adequate response to it.

The following spring, I sit in Manhattan's Riverside Park every evening and watch bearded men walk by in black hats, black suits, and white shirts without ties. They are Hasidim. No one has told me, but I know that is who they are. I stare at the older ones and imagine I see the blue-stenciled numbers on their forearms, and as I stare, I unconsciously rub my forearm. It is my suffering and theirs I want to avenge and give voice to — for them and for me.

I am obsessed by the desire to be a cantor, and sometimes when I walk past a synagogue I think I hear melodies of pain and beauty rising toward heaven.

I did not understand how that could be. But why was it necessary to understand myself? It was enough to live what had come to me to be lived.

What had come was the omnipresent subliminal awareness that six million Jews had been murdered, and not on
some day in the backwash of history. No, they were murdered while I played and while I slept, while my cousin
Dorothy was teaching the four- and five-year-old me to
read and play the piano. It did not make sense that in one
part of the world a little boy could be sitting in a library
choosing books he wanted to read, while elsewhere in the
world, at the same moment, a little boy was being murdered. But once I knew that, I could not think of my childhood without also thinking about those other little boys. I
didn't dare do otherwise.

My childhood could be true only to the extent that my
memory of it included remembering that which had happened to me though I had not seen it, smelled it, or even
known.

How do you lift a stone that weeps?

You reach down and pick it up.

4 ✧✧✧

It is important to remember that which did not happen
to me. I do that by using that most amazing of human
faculties, the imagination — that ability to experience another in myself, to experience another as myself.

As a human, I am more than I have experienced directly. If this were not so, literature, poetry, film, drama,
and so on, would not communicate to anyone except their
creators. If I were no more than *my* experience, I could not
communicate with anyone else, or they with me. Imagination is the wings of the soul, carrying me from the sin-
gularity of personal existence across the void of Time and
Space to alight in that realm where each of us is the other
and God is One.

But we seldom give the imagination a place in our reflections on history and ourselves. We seldom include it as
integral to history. We ignore that the Nazis did what they
did to the Jews because of whom they *imagined* Jews to
be.

When I confront the Holocaust, I use the faculty of
imagination because my mind is incapable of understanding death on the scale of the infinite. Imagination is the
only faculty that can bring comfort, and comfort can be
found only in choosing to live with the images of a
suffering so vast that to cry would sound like raucous
laughter.

So, the Holocaust becomes a macabre scenic backdrop
in my life, a presence that becomes a companion.

It is summer 1970. I get into the first cab waiting at the
curb outside the terminal at La Guardia, give the driver
the address of my apartment in Manhattan, and slump
into the corner of the backseat. I notice that driver looking
more at me through the rearview mirror than at the cars
he is passing with reckless confidence.

"It's you!" the cabbie finally exclaims, grinning.

It is a statement fraught with philosophical peril.

"It's you!" he repeats. "Remember me?"

I lean forward, puzzled, and look at him. After a moment, I recognize him as the same cabbie who has taken
me from La Guardia into Manhattan twice in the past
year. To get the same cabbie more than once in New York
is almost impossible; three times deserves a story in the
Daily News.

"How've you been?" he wants to know after we finish
exclaiming over the coincidence.

"Fine," I say politely. I ask about him, hoping he will
respond with equal insincerity and then leave me alone.

"You're a writer, right?" he says after a long pause.

I know what's coming: he's had a very interesting life and he knows that it would be a bestseller if he could only find somebody to write it up, and if I help him, the two of us could make a ton of money, and on and on and on.

"I've got a problem," he continues. "Maybe you can help me." There is another long pause. "I just got a letter from this cousin of mine." He stops. He opens his mouth several times, but no words come. Finally, in a gesture of desperation, he takes his right hand from the steering wheel and bends his arm back at me. I look at the numbers stenciled in blue on his forearm. "You know?"

"I know," I respond quietly.

He puts his hand back on the wheel, and the words come rapidly now. "My problem is this. I just got this letter from my cousin in Israel. She's the daughter of my mother's sister. But the problem is that for the past twenty-five years I thought everybody in my family was dead. Then last week I get this letter from her. She'd thought everybody in the family was dead, too, but somehow she heard that maybe I was alive and she got an address and wrote." He stops. "It's such a shock, you know. So, I thought since you're a writer, you could tell me what to write to her."

I slump back into the seat, my eyes shut against not only the pain and sorrow of it all, but my own impotence before the enormity of his question and the numbers on his wrist. Doesn't he see that I am black? Hasn't he read that blacks and Jews aren't allies anymore? Why ask me? And so what if I'm a writer? Only God knows what one ghost should say to another.

"Were you happy to hear from her?" I hear myself ask after a long silence.

"Oh, yes! It's a shock, but I'm very happy."

"Well, maybe that's what you should write. Tell her how happy you are."

He thinks for a moment, then looks at me in the mirror. He is smiling and nodding his head. "Thank you. That's what I'll do."

We say nothing else. I've flown into La Guardia many times since, but have never seen him again. I wonder now, was he real, or was he an angel who descended from an ash-filled sky?

There are memories, important memories, to which I cannot assign years. Why is that? Is it because an evil as enormous as the Holocaust had to have happened outside time, because history would be destroyed if it had to contain and understand such evil? Or is it that I am too small to contain evil of such breadth and therefore my contacts with the Holocaust remove me from dailiness and put me into an eternal present in which there can never be a tomorrow because the sun cannot rise or set?

It is sometime during the early seventies. One evening, I am turning the channels on the TV set, looking for something that will entertain me and allow me to forget enervating dailiness for a while.

"Sighet," the voice on the television says. It is a quiet, compelling voice. I do not know who or what Sighet is, but I am entranced by the sound of the word and the sound of the voice saying it. I sit down to watch, at least long enough to have my curiosity about Sighet satisfied.

Sighet is the name of a town in Eastern Europe, and the narrator of the film is a Jew, a survivor, who has returned to Sighet for the first time since he was transported from there to Auschwitz in 1944.

I have missed the beginning of the film and do not know who possesses that voice so filled with sorrow that my soul feels itself to be in the presence of a suffering for which there is no comfort.

When the credits are run at the end of the film, I learn whom the voice belongs to: Elie Wiesel.

In the summer of 1974, I taught summer school at Mercer University in Macon, Georgia. Most of the students in my ethnic-literature course were elementary- and junior-high-school teachers, black women and white women earning credits toward master's degrees in education. Why did I include *A Jew Today* by Elie Wiesel on the reading list? I do not know. I do not recall how I taught the book, what I said about it, or what they said about it. I only remember feeling that it was important that I include something about Jews and the Holocaust in the course because I didn't want my students to think that ethnic literature meant only blacks, Hispanics, and Native Americans.

5 ✧✧✧

Winter-spring 1979. I am on sabbatical from the university. I am planning to use the time to read recent novels by black writers and revise my Contemporary Afro-American Novel course. One January evening, I happen to pick up Raul Hilberg's *Destruction of the European Jews* from the pile of unread books stacked beside my rocking chair.

I begin reading and I cannot stop. The more I read, the more depressed I am. A depression is a hollow in the land; its root meaning is "to strike." That suggests how I feel: I have been struck so fearfully that I have fallen into a hollow in the land. I have been struck by grief and mourning for the six million murdered Jews.

Days pass. They are as heavy and silent as stones. I cook and nag the children about their chores. I shop; I watch hockey games on television with my son. I take my pregnant wife to the doctor. There are no words inside me. Only images.

I am four or five years old and come downstairs one morning and notice that the clock has stopped. Momma tells me there was a "blackout" during the night. I know it has something to do with the war, but I cannot imagine what.

I sit on the top step of the front porch of my aunt's house in Little Rock, Arkansas. I sit all day, watching army trucks and jeeps and tanks and soldiers go past. I know there is a war somewhere, but what is a war and what does a tank do?

I remember ration books. I remember buying orange stamps in school and pasting them in a book and when the book is filled, I am given a war bond. I remember sitting in the kitchen, a plastic tube filled with margarine in my hand. It is white, but at the center is a yellow globule and I press the tube until the yellow globule breaks and I squeeze the tube until the yellow color spreads through the whiteness and the margarine becomes yellow like forsythia.

The war was funerals of young men in khaki uniforms at Daddy's church; and a bronze bulletin board in the church vestibule onto which were etched the names of those killed; and little children at church on Father's Day, white flowers pinned to the lapels of their jackets or on the right shoulders of their dresses. Their fathers had died in the war and I was afraid of them.

I remember, also, my red tricycle, my doll with her blue pajamas, the pear tree in the yard whose green fruit gave me one of the worst stomachaches of my life. I remember gathering eggs in the mornings, and the bantam rooster who beat me so thoroughly and so consistently that Daddy finally had to sell the chickens. And I remember the

Saturdays, before that happened, when Daddy went into the chicken house, caught a chicken, and brought it out to the yard. Grabbing its head, he twirled his arm around and around, faster and faster, until the chicken's body flew through space and landed in the dust, where it flopped and ran with drunken steps, blood spurting from the hole where its head had been. Eventually, the headless chicken toppled over, twitching and flopping in the dust until death stilled its body. Daddy would give me the chicken's head, and after Momma scalded off the feathers and cut the chicken up, she gave me the feet. I would sit with them in the narrow alleyway between the church and the parsonage, trying to imagine what it was like to be alive and then be dead.

What was it like to be a child and inhale gas? What was it like to stand before a pit at Babi Yar and watch others being shot, knowing that within seconds you, too, would be dead, tumbling into that pit? What was it like to be that child whom an SS officer grabbed by its ankles and swung through the air in a swift arc against the side of a railroad car, the child's head and life shattering like a falling star?

Why was I alive?

Why were they dead?

I do not understand.

Chaim Kaplan, the Warsaw ghetto:

It is almost a *mitzvah* to dance. Every dance is a protest against our oppressors.

An anonymous Jew as he is being pushed into a cattle car, the Warsaw ghetto:

Jews, don't despair! Don't you realize that we are going to meet the Messiah? If I had some liquor, I'd drink a toast.

Words written on the wall of a cellar in Cologne, Germany, where Jews hid:

> I believe in the sun when it is not shining. I believe in love even when feeling it not. I believe in God even when He is silent.

I do not understand.

The more I read, the greater my numbness as I witness Jews affirming God in the midst of their own negation.

Elie Wiesel:

> They were pressed together so that they could hardly move or breathe. Suddenly an old rabbi exclaimed, "Today is Simchat Torah. Have we forgotten what Jews are ordered to do on Simchat Torah?" Somebody had managed to smuggle a small *Sefer Torah* aboard the train. He handed it to the rabbi. And they began to sing, to sway, since they could not dance. And they went on singing and celebrating the Torah, all the while knowing that every motion of the train was bringing them closer to the end.

Hermann Graebe, eyewitness to a massacre of Jews in the Ukraine in 1942:

> I watched a family of about eight persons, a man and woman, both about fifty, with their children of one, eight, and ten, and two grown-up daughters of about twenty to twenty-four. An old woman with snow-white hair was holding the one-year-old child in her arms and singing to it and tickling it. The child was cooing with delight. The couple were looking on with tears in their eyes. The father was holding the hand of a boy about ten years old and speaking to him softly; the boy was fighting his tears. The father pointed toward the sky, stroked his head and seemed

to explain something to him. At that moment the SS man at the pit shouted something to his comrade. The latter counted off about twenty persons. Among them was the family I have mentioned.

Would I be able to hold the hand of one of my children and talk of life, directing the child's eyes to the clear, blue sky so that he or she would not see the soldiers raise their rifles, so he or she would not see death? I do not know.

I awake each morning, tired. In the night, I wander among naked bodies piled atop one another; I shovel bodies into ovens and I am the Jew closing the oven door and the Jew inside; I am smoke and flame spewing from smokestacks; I am particles of ash and soul seeking my burying place in cloud and sky.

One morning, I awake and, with my eyes still closed, say to my wife, "Even God does not understand the Holocaust."

Another morning, I awake and my lips are moving. I listen. I am trying to say "*Shema Yisrael Adonai Elohenu Adonai Ehad*." At night those words resound in me and when I awake, they are the first words I hear from my lips.

I do not understand.

Some understanding comes in December 1981, when I decide to convert to Judaism. I, too, want to be one of those so in love with God that I would say the *Shema* when facing death.

6 ✧✧✧

I like stones. I used to collect them. The last time I moved, however, I found myself carrying a box of stones up from the basement. So, I don't collect them anymore.

I don't need to, now that I know that my soul is a stone, impenetrable and eternal.

My soul became a stone when I realized that God needs us. God's fate is inseparable from our own, asserted Yaakov Yosef of Polnoy. God created everything by the Word, except us. Into us He breathed His own spirit. God is dependent on us to care for that portion of His spirit that is our birthright.

If that is so, and it is, then the evil within us is from God, too. But if God and I are covenanted, and we are, then He suffers, too — from His capacity for evil as well as mine. Only to the extent that I accept this suffering can I accept God. Only to the extent that I remember the suffering of others do I remember the capacity for evil that is mine because God breathed a soul into me.

To remember. That is the key. It is not an intellectual act. It is a commitment of being. The word comes from a root that means "to mourn." How amazing! To remember is to mourn. It is an essential way by which God is known to us and we are known to ourselves. There is an old Jewish saying: "Forgetfulness leads to exile; remembering leads to redemption."

And so I remember the survivor of Treblinka who returns after the war with a group to the now-deserted death camp. They peer into the craters created by bombs dropped at the end of the war, and peering into one crater, they see human bones protruding from the dirt.

Someone points and says, "These are the bones from a child's leg!"

The survivor, a Jew who was one of only forty Jews to survive where 1.2 million were killed, rushes to the crater and pulls out the bone of a child's leg.

"There's still some flesh hanging from that leg!" someone exclaims.

The man takes a section of newspaper from someone in the group, wraps the bone in it, puts it in the breast pocket of his coat, and hugs it to himself. "Perhaps," he said, "it's the foot of my little boy whom I brought here with me."

I remember and I mourn because God should have commanded the sun to stand still in the nave of the sky until humanity mourned.

I remember with the same intensity as the Jews of Psalm 137 remembered Jerusalem. It is believed that this psalm was written sometime after the first Temple was destroyed and the Jews were forced into the *galut* of Babylon. In the Midrash on Psalms, there is this story:

> Among those carried away were the Levites, the musicians of the Temple. One evening in the midst of a large banquet, the tables laden with food and wine, the hall filled with dancing girls, King Nebuchadnezzer thought to heighten the evening's entertainment by having the Levites brought to him. He commanded them to play their instruments and sing the Lord's songs for him as they had done in the Temple. There was great applause and laughter from the Babylonians feasting themselves. When the laughter stopped and the hall was quiet, the Levites stood up and each man put his thumb in his mouth and broke it.

Remembering is not only to be carried on the scarlet wings of the imagination through the void of Time and Space. Remembering is also the act of total and singular commitment to myself as the silence in which God dwells. Such a commitment might require me to break my thumb rather than forget you, O Jerusalem!

Such a commitment also requires me to know that remembering is not only composed of mourning and sorrow; there is another emotion, too — anger. Psalm 137 states it forcefully.

> O, Babylon, Babylon the destroyer,
> A blessing on him
>   who repays you for all that you did to us!
> A blessing on him
>   who seizes your children and
>   dashes them against the rocks!

There are times when anger and, yes, even hatred can be holy. Interestingly enough, another of the roots of the word *remember* is in the name of the Old Norse god Mimir, "a giant who guards the well of wisdom."

How often I feel within me an anger so enormous and so fierce that it feels like a giant that will devour me. Anger of such proportions is frightening, and I fear that if I give in to it I will be seized by a giant who will plunge me deeper and deeper into some depth where I will drown. Suffering can be like this, too. But it is not a drowning that anger would lead me to. The giants of anger and suffering guard the well of wisdom.

To remember the Holocaust is not only to mourn; it is also to be enraged. It is to stand naked beneath the sky, shake my fist at heaven, and demand that God bless "him who seizes your children and dashes them against the rocks."

Just as it was not right or possible for the Jews in their Babylonian exile not to feel rage at the destruction of Jerusalem and the Temple, it is not right if I do not feel rage for the murders of those six million women, men, and children.

When I truly meet the giant guarding the well of wisdom, when I allow myself the rage as well as the sorrow, the tears as well as the desire for vengeance — and the desire is not the same as the act — then, and only then, do I lower my bucket into the well of wisdom.

7 ✧✧✧

R. Abbahu said:

God mourned only over the heart of man, as one does who has made something bad, and knows that he has not made a good thing, and says, "What have I made?" So God said: "It was I who put the bad leaven in the dough, for the *yetzer* of the heart of man is evil from his youth." God grieved over man's heart.

That is the antidote to evil. I must grieve over the hearts of us all. I must grieve so loudly that my grief becomes a prayer. I must utter no words asking for forgiveness, but let my grief be the forgiveness. If God grieves over my heart for having created me with the *yetzer*, then I must grieve for God for having created the *yetzer*.

Evil is. That is the unmistakable message of the Holocaust. Look and see what evil is capable of. Evil is. Until I accept this, I cannot accept that I am human. I cannot accept God as God.

In the Mishnah Berakhot are these words:

A man must recite a benediction for evil, just as he recites a benediction for good. For it is said: "And thou shalt love the Lord thy God with all thy heart, and with all thy soul, and with all thy might." "With all thy heart" — with thy two wills, with thy will to good and thy will to evil.

God is to be loved with the *yezer ha-Ra*, too. I cannot truly love if I omit from that love my capacity for evil. If

God loves me by His grief, than it is with my grief that I must love.

Isn't that what I am called to by the Holocaust — to love by grieving. I am not called to understand. I am not called to speculate on the concept of God after Auschwitz. I am not called to be rational in any way. I am called to remember — that is, to mourn and to grieve and to bring into my soul the evil that is.

This is the stone my soul is becoming. It is a stone that weeps. It is a stone that bleeds.

It is my offering to God

and

you.